most loved recipe collection most loved recipe collection

most loved soups

Pictured on front cover:
Cream of Carrot Soup, page 88

Pictured on back cover:
Hot and Sour Turkey Pot Soup, page 36

Most Loved Soups
Copyright © Company's Coming Publishing Limited

All rights reserved worldwide. No part of this book may be reproduced, stored in a retrieval system or transmitted in any form by any means without written permission in advance from the publisher.

In the case of photocopying or other reprographic copying, a license may be purchased from the Canadian Copyright Licensing Agency (Access Copyright). Visit www.accesscopyright.ca or call toll free 1-800-893-5777. In the United States, please contact the Copyright Clearance Centre at www.copyright.com or call 978-646-8600.

Brief portions of this book may be reproduced for review purposes, provided credit is given to the source. Reviewers are invited to contact the publisher for additional information.

First Printing November 2011

Library and Archives Canada Cataloguing in Publication
Paré, Jean, date
Most loved soups / Jean Paré.
   (Most loved recipe collection)
Includes index.
ISBN 978-1-897477-33-5
   1. Soups. I. Title. II. Series: Paré, Jean, date. Most loved recipe collection.
TX757.P363 2010   641.8'13   C2009-906136-8

Published by
Company's Coming Publishing Limited
2311 – 96 Street
Edmonton, Alberta, Canada T6N 1G3
Tel: 780-450-6223   Fax: 780-450-1857
www.companyscoming.com

Company's Coming is a registered trademark owned by Company's Coming Publishing Limited

We acknowledge the financial support of the Government of Canada through the Canada Book Fund for our publishing activities.

Printed in Malaysia

We gratefully acknowledge the following suppliers for their generous support of our Test and Photography Kitchens:

Broil King Barbecues
Corelle®
Hamilton Beach® Canada
Lagostina®
Proctor Silex® Canada
Tupperware®

Our special thanks to the following business for providing props for photography:

Stokes

Pictured from left: Coconut Shrimp Soup, page 41; Scotch Broth, page 75;
Pineapple Mango Soup and West Indies Summer Soup, page 118; Sweet Potato Vichyssoise, page 106

table of contents

the Company's Coming story

"Never share a recipe you wouldn't use yourself."

Jean Paré (pronounced "jeen PAIR-ee") grew up understanding that the combination of family, friends and home cooking is the best recipe for a good life. From her mother, she learned to appreciate good cooking, while her father praised even her earliest attempts in the kitchen. When Jean left home, she took with her a love of cooking, many family recipes and an intriguing desire to read cookbooks as if they were novels!

When her four children had all reached school age, Jean volunteered to cater the 50th anniversary celebration of the Vermilion School of Agriculture, now Lakeland College, in Alberta, Canada. Working out of her home, Jean prepared a dinner for more than 1,000 people, launching a flourishing catering operation that continued for over 18 years. During that time, she had countless opportunities to test new ideas with immediate feedback—resulting in empty plates and contented customers! Whether preparing cocktail sandwiches for a house party or serving a hot meal for 1,500 people, Jean Paré earned a reputation for great food, courteous service and reasonable prices.

As requests for her recipes increased, Jean was often asked the question, "Why don't you write a cookbook?" Jean responded by teaming up with her son, Grant Lovig, in the fall of 1980 to form Company's Coming Publishing Limited. The publication of *150 Delicious Squares* on April 14, 1981 marked the debut of what would soon become one of the world's most popular cookbook series.

The company has grown since those early days when Jean worked from a spare bedroom in her home. Today, she continues to write recipes while working closely with the staff of the Recipe Factory, as the Company's Coming test kitchen is affectionately known. There she fills the role of mentor, assisting with the development of recipes people most want to use for everyday cooking and easy entertaining. Every Company's Coming recipe is *kitchen-tested* before it is approved for publication.

Jean's daughter, Gail Lovig, is responsible for marketing and distribution, leading a team that includes sales personnel located in major cities across Canada. Company's Coming cookbooks are distributed in Canada, the United States, Australia and other world markets. Bestsellers many times over in English, Company's Coming cookbooks have also been published in French and Spanish.

Familiar and trusted in home kitchens around the world, Company's Coming cookbooks are offered in a variety of formats. Highly regarded as kitchen workbooks, the softcover Original Series, with its lay-flat plastic comb binding, is still a favourite among readers.

Jean Paré's approach to cooking has always called for *quick and easy recipes* using *everyday ingredients.* That view has served her well. The recipient of many awards, including the Queen Elizabeth Golden Jubilee Medal, Jean was appointed Member of the Order of Canada, her country's highest lifetime achievement honour.

Jean continues to gain new supporters by adhering to what she calls The Golden Rule of Cooking: *Never share a recipe you wouldn't use yourself.* It's an approach that has worked—*millions of times over!*

foreword

Homemade soups radiate comfort, and tucking into a bowl can brighten an otherwise grey day. The aroma of a simmering pot of homemade soup has the power to bring back all kinds of memories and make us feel relaxed and happy. In this new collection of soups, we've selected all of our favourite soup recipes from the Company's Coming library so you'll have the best of the best in one handy volume.

Soup isn't just about comfort though. Light, clear soups such as Beef Wine Consommé make elegant dinner starters. Chilled savoury soups like Gazpacho or Vichyssoise work well as refreshing and light summer meals. Hearty Minestrone and Manhattan Clam Chowder are nutritious meals in a bowl. And chilled sweet soups such as Cherry Soup make for delicious and novel desserts. One of the great things about soup is how varied it can be and how well it can fit into any menu.

In *Most Loved Soups* you'll find not only a wide range of delicious soup recipes to choose from, but also two flavourful stock recipes, one for beef (page 6) and one for chicken (page 26), which can be used to make many of the other soups in the book. By making large batches of these two recipes periodically, and then freezing them, you'll have the base for all kinds of other great soups on hand. Add some noodles to the stocks themselves and you'll have light, heartwarming soups sure to make you feel better.

Making soup at home allows you to select more healthful ingredients and control the salt and fat in what you eat. Much of the fat in stock, or any broth-based soup, can be removed by skimming it off the surface. Puréeing or adding potatoes or onions will thicken a soup without the need to add cream. Using reduced-sodium prepared broths or making your own stock at home helps control salt levels. Adding beans and legumes increases protein, fibre and nutrients while adding minimal calories, salt and fat.

Discover the wonders of soups with *Most Loved Soups* and you'll be sitting down to a steaming, delicious bowl of something "souper" before you know it!

Jean Paré

nutrition information

Each recipe is analyzed using the most current version of the Canadian Nutrient File from Health Canada, which is based on the United States Department of Agriculture (USDA) Nutrient Database.

- If more than one ingredient is listed (such as "butter or hard margarine"), or if a range is given (1 – 2 tsp., 5 – 10 mL), only the first ingredient or first amount is analyzed.

- For meat, poultry and fish, the serving size per person is based on the recommended 4 oz. (113 g) uncooked weight (without bone), which is 2 – 3 oz. (57 – 85 g) cooked weight (without bone)— approximately the size of a deck of playing cards.

- Milk used is 1% M.F. (milk fat), unless otherwise stated.

- Cooking oil used is canola oil, unless otherwise stated.

- Ingredients indicating "sprinkle," "optional," or "for garnish" are not included in the nutrition information.

- The fat in recipes and combination foods can vary greatly depending on the sources and types of fats used in each specific ingredient. For these reasons, the amount of saturated, monounsaturated and polyunsaturated fats may not add up to the total fat content.

Vera C. Mazurak, Ph.D.
Nutritionist

Good things come to those who wait, and a long simmering time really brings out the flavour in this beef barley soup. The beef bones make this stock deliciously rich and savoury.

about stock

There are several different sources of broth if you don't have the time to make your own stock. Store-bought broth comes in a ready-to-use form in cans or cartons. You can also mix bouillon cubes, pastes or powders with hot water to create instant broth in a pinch. For any recipe in this book that requires stock, you may use either store-bought broth or homemade stock. However, if you're concerned about keeping your salt intake low, then homemade stock is preferable to store-bought broths. For more stock tips, see page 26.

Old-Fashioned Barley Soup

A Classic!

BEEF STOCK

Beef neck bones	3 lbs.	1.4 kg
Bone-in beef shanks	1 lb.	454 g
Cold water	16 cups	4 L
Celery ribs, with leaves, halved	6	6
Medium onions, halved	2	2
Medium carrot, halved	1	1
Bay leaves	2	2
Whole black peppercorns	10	10

SOUP

Diced peeled potato	2 cups	500 mL
Can of condensed tomato soup	10 oz.	284 mL
Chopped onion	1 cup	250 mL
Chopped celery	1 cup	250 mL
Diced carrot	1 cup	250 mL
Diced parsnip (optional)	1 cup	250 mL
Pearl barley	2/3 cup	150 mL
Salt	1 tsp.	5 mL
Pepper	3/4 tsp.	4 mL

Beef Stock: Put first 3 ingredients into large pot. Bring to a boil. Boil, uncovered, for 5 minutes without stirring. Skim and discard foam from side of pot.

Add next 5 ingredients. Stir. Reduce heat to medium-low. Simmer, partially covered, for about 4 hours, stirring occasionally, until beef starts to fall off bones. Remove from heat. Remove bones and shanks to cutting board using slotted spoon. Remove beef from bones. Discard bones. Chop beef coarsely. Set aside. Strain stock through sieve into separate large pot. Discard solids. Makes about 10 cups (2.5 L) stock.

Soup: Add remaining 9 ingredients to stock in pot. Bring to a boil. Add beef. Reduce heat to medium-low. Simmer, partially covered, for about 45 minutes, stirring occasionally, until barley and vegetables are tender. Makes about 14 cups (3.5 L).

1 cup (250 mL): 112 Calories; 2.1 g Total Fat (0.8 g Mono, 0.3 g Poly, 0.7 g Sat); 11 mg Cholesterol; 17 g Carbohydrate; 2 g Fibre; 6 g Protein; 345 mg Sodium

Pictured at right.

Tender beef and plenty of vegetables pair up in a dark, flavourful broth. This is a small-batch recipe, but it's easily doubled.

Beefy Vegetable Soup

Boneless beef, such as stew beef, diced	1/4 lb.	113 g
Water	3 cups	750 mL
Chopped onion	1/2 cup	125 mL
Medium carrot, diced	1	1
Diced turnip	1/3 cup	75 mL
Beef bouillon powder	1 tbsp.	15 mL
Small bay leaf	1	1
Parsley flakes, sprinkle		
Ground sage, sprinkle		
Pepper, sprinkle		

Cook beef in water slowly in covered saucepan for 1 hour.

Add remaining 8 ingredients. Cover. Boil gently for about 30 minutes until vegetables are tender. Discard bay leaf. Makes about 4 cups (1 L).

1 cup (250 mL): 77 Calories; 3.9 g Total Fat (1.7 g Mono, 0.2 g Poly, 1.5 g Sat); 18 mg Cholesterol; 5 g Carbohydrate; 1 g Fibre; 6 g Protein; 828 mg Sodium

Hearty vegetables and a robust tomato herb broth transform hamburger into a marvelous meal, ready in less than an hour!

make ahead

This soup freezes well, so pop some lunch-size portions in the freezer.

Hamburger Soup

A Classic!

Cooking oil	1 tsp.	5 mL
Lean ground beef	1 lb.	454 g
Chopped onion	1 cup	250 mL
Diced carrot	1 cup	250 mL
Chopped celery	1/2 cup	125 mL
Can of diced tomatoes (with juice)	14 oz.	398 mL
Water	1 1/2 cups	375 mL
Can of condensed beef broth	10 oz.	284 mL
Frozen kernel corn	1 cup	250 mL
Can of tomato sauce	7 1/2 oz.	213 mL
Granulated sugar	1 tsp.	5 mL
Worcestershire sauce	1 tsp.	5 mL
Dried basil (optional)	1/2 – 1 tsp.	2 – 5 mL
Pepper	1/4 tsp.	1 mL

(continued on next page)

Heat cooking oil in large saucepan on medium. Add ground beef. Scramble-fry for about 5 minutes until no longer pink. Drain.

Add onion, carrot and celery. Cook for about 5 minutes, stirring often, until onion is softened.

Add remaining 9 ingredients. Stir. Bring to a boil on medium-high. Reduce heat to medium-low. Cover. Simmer for about 45 minutes until vegetables are tender. Makes about 6 3/4 cups (1.7 L).

1 cup (250 mL): 183 Calories; 6.9 g Total Fat (3.0 g Mono, 0.6 g Poly, 2.4 g Sat); 35 mg Cholesterol; 16 g Carbohydrate; 3 g Fibre; 16 g Protein; 634 mg Sodium

Pictured below.   Hamburger Soup, left

A satisfying and full-bodied soup that makes a real meal! Beef stock can be used in place of the bouillon cubes and water, and a can of chickpeas (garbanzo beans) can be used instead of kidney beans.

about minestrone

Minestra (mee-NES-trah) is the Italian word for soup, usually one of medium thickness containing meat and vegetables. *Minestrina* (mee-nes-TREE-nah), or "little soup," is a light broth containing thin or small pasta. *Minestrone* (mee-nes-TROH-neh), or "big soup," is filled with vegetables, pasta, meat and beans and intended to be a meal in a bowl.

freezing

This recipe makes a big batch of soup, but leftovers can be frozen.

Minestrone

A Classic!

Bacon slices, chopped	4	4
Chopped onion	1 1/2 cups	375 mL
Lean ground beef	1 1/2 lbs.	680 g
Beef bouillon cubes	10 x 1/5 oz.	10 x 6 g
Boiling water	10 cups	2.5 L
Can of plum tomatoes, broken up	14 oz.	398 mL
Chopped celery	1 cup	250 mL
Diced carrot	1 cup	250 mL
Diced potato	1 1/2 cups	375 mL
Chopped cabbage, packed	1 cup	250 mL
Salt	1 tsp.	5 mL
Pepper	1/4 tsp.	1 mL
Garlic powder	1/4 tsp.	1 mL
Dried basil	1/2 tsp.	2 mL
Dried oregano	1/2 tsp.	2 mL
Fusilli	8 oz.	225 g
Can of kidney beans, rinsed and drained	14 oz.	398 mL

Scramble-fry bacon, onion and ground beef in Dutch oven to brown.

Dissolve bouillon cubes in boiling water. Add.

Add next 10 ingredients. Stir. Bring to a boil. Cover and simmer until vegetables are tender, about 25 minutes.

Add pasta and beans. Boil slowly, uncovered, for 10 minutes or until pasta is tender. Makes about 14 cups (3.5 L).

*1 cup (**250 mL**): 259 Calories; 10.8 g Total Fat (1.4 g Mono, 0.4 g Poly, 4.0 g Sat); 38 mg Cholesterol; 25 g Carbohydrate; 3 g Fibre; 15 g Protein; 1352 mg Sodium*

Italian Meatball Soup

Large egg	1	1
Crushed seasoned croutons	1/4 cup	60 mL
Chopped fresh parsley	2 tbsp.	30 mL
(or 1 1/2 tsp., 7 mL, flakes)		
Grated Parmesan cheese	2 tbsp.	30 mL
Garlic clove, minced	1	1
(or 1/4 tsp., 1 mL, powder)		
Lean ground beef	1 lb.	454 g
Prepared beef broth	7 cups	1.75 L
Very small pasta (such as orzo	2/3 cup	150 mL
or alphabet)		
Finely shredded fresh basil	2 tbsp.	30 mL

Combine first 5 ingredients in medium bowl.

Add ground beef. Mix well. Roll into 3/4 inch (2 cm) balls. Arrange on greased baking sheet with sides. Bake in 350°F (175°C) oven for about 15 minutes until no longer pink inside. Makes about 65 meatballs. Transfer to paper towels to drain. Set aside.

Measure broth into large pot or Dutch oven. Bring to a boil on high. Add pasta. Stir. Reduce heat to medium. Boil gently, uncovered, for 5 to 6 minutes until pasta is tender but firm.

Add meatballs and basil. Heat and stir for about 1 minute until meatballs are heated through. Makes about 8 cups (2 L).

1 cup (250 mL): 209 Calories; 7.1 g Total Fat (2.9 g Mono, 0.5 g Poly, 2.8 g Sat); 58 mg Cholesterol; 18 g Carbohydrate; 1 g Fibre; 17 g Protein; 817 mg Sodium

This tasty soup is a creative way to serve pasta with meatballs.

food fun

Some call Italian Meatball Soup by another name, Italian Wedding Soup, although it's not a dish traditionally served at Italian weddings. Food historians think the name came from the idea that the meat, cheese, pasta and herbs in the soup create a marriage of delicious flavours!

A meal in a bowl. Sweet tomato broth with a dash of Parmesan cheese that will have everyone returning for seconds. A great choice for an Italian potluck.

Meatball Soup

Large egg	1	1
Lean ground beef	1 lb.	454 g
Long-grain white rice	1/4 cup	60 mL
Dried oregano	1/2 tsp.	2 mL
Cooking oil	2 tsp.	10 mL
Cooking oil	1 tsp.	5 mL
Diced carrot	1 cup	250 mL
Chopped onion	1/2 cup	125 mL
Water	2 cups	500 mL
Can of condensed tomato soup	10 oz.	284 mL
Prepared beef broth	1 cup	250 mL
Frozen peas	1/2 cup	125 mL
Grated Parmesan cheese	1/4 cup	60 mL

Beat egg with fork in large bowl. Add ground beef, rice and oregano. Mix well. Roll into 1/2 inch (12 mm) balls.

(continued on next page)

Meatball Soup, above

Heat first amount of cooking oil in large saucepan on medium. Add meatballs. Cook for about 10 minutes, turning occasionally, until browned. Makes about 70 meatballs. Transfer to paper towels to drain.

Heat second amount of cooking oil in same large saucepan on medium. Add carrot and onion. Cook for 5 to 10 minutes, stirring often, until onion is softened.

Add next 3 ingredients. Stir. Add meatballs. Stir. Bring to a boil on medium-high. Reduce heat to medium-low. Cover. Simmer for about 30 minutes, stirring occasionally, until meatballs are no longer pink inside and rice is tender.

Add peas and Parmesan cheese. Heat and stir for about 2 minutes until heated through. Makes about 6 cups (1.5 L).

1 cup (250 mL): 293 Calories; 16.9 g Total Fat (7.2 g Mono, 1.8 g Poly, 6.0 g Sat); 82 mg Cholesterol; 15 g Carbohydrate; 2 g Fibre; 20 g Protein; 663 mg Sodium

Pictured at left.

Beef Wine Consommé

Water	3 cups	750 mL
Onion slivers	1 tbsp.	15 mL
Carrot slivers	1 tbsp.	15 mL
Celery slivers	1 tbsp.	15 mL
Yellow turnip (or parsnip) slivers	1 tbsp.	15 mL
Chopped green onion	1 tbsp.	15 mL
Beef bouillon powder	1 tbsp.	15 mL
Granulated sugar	1 1/2 tsp.	7 mL
Lemon juice	1/2 tsp.	2 mL
Salt	1/4 tsp.	1 mL
Dry red (or alcohol-free) wine	1/4 cup	60 mL

Place first 6 ingredients in medium saucepan. Bring to a boil. Cover. Simmer for about 5 minutes until vegetables are cooked.

Add remaining 5 ingredients. Stir. Simmer for about 1 minute. Makes 3 cups (750 mL). Serves 4.

1 serving: 26 Calories; 0.2 g Total Fat (0.1 g Mono, trace Poly, 0.1 g Sat); trace Cholesterol; 3 g Carbohydrate; race Fibre; trace Protein; 950 mg Sodium

A clear, richly flavoured starter soup with elegant vegetable slivers and a hint of red wine. This is easy to double to make more servings.

about consommé

Traditionally, consommé (CON- so-may) is a rich broth that can be served hot or cold or as a base for other soups or sauces. Double consommé is broth that has been reduced by half the volume, and as a result, it has twice the flavour of non- reduced consommé.

Ban-foh-BOH is a common meal served in all Vietnamese homes. Street vendors in larger cities have this beef noodle soup available all day. Very good.

food fun

Believe it or not, there's an art to eating pho! Begin with a pair of chopsticks and a Chinese-style soup spoon. First add more garnishes to your soup such as basil or mint leaves, bean sprouts, cilantro and fresh chili peppers. Then add squirts of lime juice and fish sauce (hoisin or plum sauce are nice additions too). Using your chopsticks, pile some rice noodles, a piece of meat, some herbs and sprouts and a little broth onto the spoon, and then deliver the savoury bundle to your mouth.

Banh Pho Bo

Diced onion	1 cup	250 mL
Cooking oil	1 tbsp.	15 mL
Finely grated ginger root (or 1/2 tsp., 2 mL, ground ginger)	2 tsp.	10 mL
Garlic clove, minced (or 1/4 tsp., 1 mL, powder)	1	1
Freshly ground pepper, sprinkle		
Ground cinnamon, sprinkle		
Cans of condensed chicken broth (10 oz., 284 mL, each)	2	2
Water	3 cups	750 mL
Beef bouillon powder	2 tsp.	10 mL
Grated carrot	1/2 cup	125 mL
Fresh small red chili (seeds and ribs removed for less heat), finely diced (see Tip, right)	1	1
Fish sauce	3 tbsp.	50 mL
Lime juice	1 tbsp.	15 mL
Beef tenderloin, very thinly sliced across the grain (see Tip, page 16)	5 oz.	140 g
Green onions, cut into 1 1/2 inch (3.8 cm) pieces and then cut julienne (see Tip, page 60)	2	2
Fresh bean sprouts	3 oz.	85 g
Small rice stick noodles	8 oz.	225 g
Boiling water, to cover		
Shredded fresh basil (or cilantro), for garnish		

(continued on next page)

Sauté onion in cooking oil in large saucepan for about 3 minutes until soft.

Add ginger, garlic, pepper and cinnamon. Stir. Sauté for 3 minutes until onion is browned.

Add next 5 ingredients. Stir. Reduce heat. Cover. Simmer for 10 minutes.

Add fish sauce, lime juice, beef, green onion and bean sprouts. Stir. Bring to a simmer. Simmer until beef is cooked. Turn off heat. Cover to keep hot. Makes 7 cups (1.75 L) soup.

Cover noodles with boiling water in large heatproof bowl. Let stand for 3 minutes until softened. Drain. Divide noodles among 6 large individual soup bowls. Ladle soup over top.

Garnish with basil. Serves 6.

1 serving: 241 Calories; 4.5 g Total Fat (1.8 g Mono, 0.8 g Poly, 0.6 g Sat); 17 mg Cholesterol; 41 g Carbohydrate; 2 g Fibre; 9 g Protein; 1756 mg Sodium

Pictured below.

tip

Hot peppers contain capsaicin in the seeds and ribs. Removing the seeds and ribs will reduce the heat. Wear rubber gloves when handling hot peppers and avoid touching your eyes. Wash your hands well afterwards.

This quick soup is hearty, fragrant and just spicy enough! Make it a meal with bread sticks or a warm loaf of crusty bread.

tip

To slice meat easily, freeze for about 30 minutes and then partially thaw before slicing.

Curried Lentil Beef Soup

Cooking oil	1 tbsp.	15 mL
Beef minute (or fast-fry) steak, thinly sliced (see Tip, left)	1/2 lb.	225 g
Chopped onion	1 1/2 cups	375 mL
Curry paste	2 tbsp.	30 mL
Prepared beef broth	6 cups	1.5 L
Can of lentils, rinsed and drained	19 oz.	540 mL
Frozen mixed vegetables	1 1/2 cups	375 mL
Pepper, sprinkle		

Heat cooking oil in large pot or Dutch oven on medium-high. Add steak. Cook for 4 to 5 minutes, stirring occasionally, until browned.

Add onion and curry paste. Heat and stir for 1 minute until fragrant.

Add broth and lentils. Stir. Bring to a boil. Reduce heat to medium-low. Cover. Simmer for 5 minutes, stirring occasionally, to blend flavours.

Add mixed vegetables and pepper. Stir. Bring to a boil on high. Reduce heat to medium. Cover. Simmer for about 5 minutes until vegetables are tender. Makes about 9 cups (2.25 L).

1 cup (250 mL): 132 Calories; 3.3 g Total Fat (1.7 g Mono, 0.6 g Poly, 0.8 g Sat); 15 mg Cholesterol; 14 g Carbohydrate; 5 g Fibre; 12 g Protein; 731 mg Sodium

Pictured at right.

Earthy mushrooms and a pleasant hint of tarragon complement the nutty flavour of wild rice. Delicious.

Hearty Wild Rice Soup

Cooking oil	2 tsp.	10 mL
Chopped fresh white mushrooms	2 cups	500 mL
Lean ground beef	1 lb.	454 g
Chopped onion	1 cup	250 mL
Dried tarragon	1 tsp.	5 mL
All-purpose flour	3 tbsp.	50 mL
Prepared beef broth	6 cups	1.5 L
Wild rice	2/3 cup	150 mL
Grated carrot	1/2 cup	125 mL

(continued on next page)

Heat cooking oil in large pot or Dutch oven on medium. Add next 4 ingredients. Scramble-fry for about 10 minutes until ground beef is no longer pink. Drain.

Add flour. Stir well. Add broth and rice. Stir until boiling. Reduce heat to medium-low. Simmer, covered, for about 50 minutes, stirring occasionally, until rice is tender.

Add carrot. Heat and stir for about 2 minutes until carrot is tender-crisp. Skim any fat from surface of soup. Makes about 8 cups (2 L).

1 cup (250 mL): 187 Calories; 6.6 g Total Fat (2.9 g Mono, 0.7 g Poly, 2.2 g Sat); 29 mg Cholesterol; 16 g Carbohydrate; 2 g Fibre; 15 g Protein; 646 mg Sodium

Pictured below.

Left: Curried Lentil Beef Soup, left
Right: Hearty Wild Rice Soup, left

about wild rice

Wild rice is not a true rice, but the seed of a grass that grows naturally in the shallow waters and slow-flowing streams of temperate climates. Saskatchewan, California and Minnesota are the largest North American producers of wild rice today, but Native Americans have been harvesting the seed heads for centuries. Its distinctive nutty flavour, chewy texture and high nutritional value make wild rice a very healthy choice, and it tastes great mixed with other rices.

This rich broth seasoned with cumin and coriander provides a spicy taste of the East.

serving suggestion

For an authentic Indian touch, serve with pappadums (PAH-pah-duhms)—thin cracker-type bread made with lentil flour.

Spiced Beef Soup

Cooking oil	1 tbsp.	15 mL
Beef stew meat, cut into 1/2 inch (12 mm) pieces	3/4 lb.	340 g
Cooking oil	2 tsp.	10 mL
Chopped onion	1 1/2 cups	375 mL
Ground cumin	2 tsp.	10 mL
Ground coriander	2 tsp.	10 mL
Ground ginger	1 tsp.	5 mL
Dried crushed chilies	1 tsp.	5 mL
Can of diced tomatoes (with juice)	28 oz.	796 mL
Low-sodium prepared beef broth	4 cups	1 L
Can of chickpeas (garbanzo beans), rinsed and drained	19 oz.	540 mL
Medium zucchini (with peel), chopped	1	1
Chopped fresh mint leaves (or 1 1/2 tsp., 7 mL, dried)	2 tbsp.	30 mL
Liquid honey	2 tsp.	10 mL
Grated lemon zest	1 tsp.	5 mL

Heat first amount of cooking oil in large pot or Dutch oven on medium-high. Add beef. Cook for 5 to 10 minutes, stirring occasionally, until browned. Transfer to large bowl. Cover to keep warm.

Heat second amount of cooking oil in same large pot on medium. Add onion. Cook for 5 to 10 minutes, stirring often, until softened.

Add next 4 ingredients. Heat and stir for about 1 minute until fragrant.

Add beef, tomatoes and broth. Stir. Bring to a boil on medium-high. Reduce heat to medium-low. Cover. Simmer for 20 minutes, stirring occasionally.

(continued on next page)

Add chickpeas. Stir. Cover. Simmer for about 20 minutes until beef is very tender.

Add remaining 4 ingredients. Stir. Cook, uncovered, on medium for about 5 minutes until zucchini is tender. Makes 10 cups (2.5 L) Serves 8.

1 serving: 200 Calories; 7.9 g Total Fat (3.5 g Mono, 1.5 g Poly, 1.8 g Sat); 24 mg Cholesterol; 19 g Carbohydrate; 3 g Fibre; 15 g Protein; 605 mg Sodium

Pictured below.

Wholesome tomatoes and potatoes in a simple beef broth.

about paprika

Made from dried sweet red peppers, paprika is often associated with Hungary, where it is used extensively to flavour foods. It's also produced in Spain. Hungarian paprika is made from a variety of peppers and ranges from mild and sweet to hot and spicy. In Spain, the peppers are often smoked before being ground up, producing a paprika with an intense smoky quality. Try a specialty food store for the best selection.

variation

We used regular paprika in this dish, but for a more intense flavour, try using authentic hot Hungarian paprika.

Goulash Chowder

Chopped onion	1/2 cup	125 mL
Cooking oil	1 tbsp.	15 mL
All-purpose flour	2 tbsp.	30 mL
Boneless beef inside round (or blade or chuck) steak, trimmed of fat and cubed	3/4 lb.	340 g
Water	4 cups	1 L
Medium potatoes, diced	4	4
Can of diced tomatoes, with juice	14 oz.	398 mL
Frozen kernel corn	1/2 cup	125 mL
Paprika	1/2 – 1 tsp.	2 – 5 mL
Granulated sugar	1/2 tsp.	2 mL
Salt	1 tsp.	5 mL
Pepper	1/4 tsp.	1 mL

Sauté onion in cooking oil in large pot or Dutch oven until soft and golden. Stir in flour until well mixed. Turn into small bowl. Set aside.

Put beef and water into same pot. Cover. Simmer for 1 to 1 1/2 hours until tender.

Add next 7 ingredients. Cook for 25 minutes. Add reserved onion mixture. Heat and stir until boiling and thickened. Makes 9 cups (2.25 L).

1 cup (250 mL): 151 Calories; 5.6 g Total Fat (2.5 g Mono, 0.7 g Poly, 1.6 g Sat); 25 mg Cholesterol; 17 g Carbohydrate; 2 g Fibre; 10 g Protein; 390 mg Sodium

Pictured at right.

Why wait until Sunday for a pot roast dinner? This rich, stew-like soup is full of tender meat and vegetables for that feeling of savoury satisfaction, any day of the week.

tip

Try freezing tomato paste for 30 minutes before opening both ends and pushing the tube out. You'll be able to slice off what you need and wrap the rest for later.

Pot Roast Soup

Cooking oil	2 tsp.	10 mL
Beef top sirloin steak, trimmed of fat and diced	1 lb.	454 g
Chopped onion	1 cup	250 mL
Garlic cloves, minced (or 1/2 tsp., 2 mL, powder)	2	2
Beef Stock (page 6), or prepared beef broth	5 cups	1.25 L
Cubed peeled potato	2 cups	500 mL
Baby carrots, halved	1 cup	250 mL
Tomato paste (see Tip, left)	1 tbsp.	15 mL
Worcestershire sauce	1 tbsp.	15 mL
Dried thyme	1/4 tsp.	1 mL
Salt	1/4 tsp.	1 mL
Water	1/4 cup	60 mL
All-purpose flour	1/4 cup	60 mL
Frozen peas	1 cup	250 mL

Heat cooking oil in large saucepan on medium-high. Add beef. Cook for about 10 minutes, stirring often, until browned. Reduce heat to medium.

Add onion and garlic. Cook for 3 to 5 minutes, stirring occasionally, until onion is softened.

Add stock. Stir. Bring to a boil. Reduce heat to medium-low. Simmer, partially covered, for about 40 minutes until beef is tender.

Add next 6 ingredients. Bring to a boil.

Stir water into flour in small bowl until smooth. Slowly add to soup, stirring constantly, until boiling and thickened. Reduce heat to medium. Boil gently, covered, for 15 to 20 minutes, stirring occasionally, until vegetables are tender.

Add peas. Heat and stir for 3 to 5 minutes until peas are tender. Makes 8 cups (2 L). Serves 6.

1 serving: 233 Calories; 4.8 g Total Fat (2.1 g Mono, 0.7 g Poly, 1.2 g Sat); 36 mg Cholesterol; 24 g Carbohydrate; 3 g Fibre; 23 g Protein; 931 mg Sodium

Pictured at right.

This soup hearty with pasta, beef and navy beans (fah-JOH-lee) is filling, easy to prepare and delicious—sure to become a favourite!

food fun

Anyone who remembers the Dean Martin classic *That's Amore* may recall a line in the song where he mentions Pasta Fagioli, except in his version, it's called "pasta fazool" and eating it puts you in a state similar to being in love!

variation

In place of navy beans you can use white kidney beans, mixed beans, black-eyed peas or another bean of your choice.

Pasta Fagioli Soup

Olive (or cooking) oil	1 tbsp.	15 mL
Medium onion, chopped	1	1
Celery rib, finely diced	1	1
Garlic clove, minced	1	1
(or 1/4 tsp., 1 mL, powder)		
Extra lean ground beef	6 oz.	170 g
All-purpose flour	1 tsp.	5 mL
Salt	1/2 tsp.	2 mL
Coarse ground pepper	1/2 tsp.	2 mL
Cayenne pepper (optional)	1/8 tsp.	0.5 mL
Prepared beef broth	3 2/3 cups	900 mL
Cans of stewed tomatoes	2	2
(14 oz., 398 mL, each)		
Can of vegetable cocktail juice	12 oz.	340 mL
Coarsely grated carrot	1/2 cup	125 mL
Dried basil	1 tsp.	5 mL
Granulated sugar	1/4 tsp.	1 mL
Cans of navy beans (14 oz., 398 mL, each), rinsed and drained	2	2
Leftover cooked pasta, chopped if long or very large	1 cup	250 mL

Heat olive oil in large pot or Dutch oven on medium. Add onion, celery and garlic. Cook for 5 to 10 minutes, stirring often, until onion and celery are softened.

Add ground beef. Scramble-fry for about 10 minutes until no longer pink.

Add next 4 ingredients. Stir.

Add next 6 ingredients. Stir.

(continued on next page)

Mash 1/2 cup (125 mL) beans in small bowl. Add to pot. Add remaining beans to pot. Bring to a boil. Reduce heat to medium-low. Simmer, uncovered, for 15 minutes.

Add pasta. Simmer, uncovered, for about 5 minutes until heated through. Makes 12 cups (3 L).

1 cup (250 mL): 314 Calories; 3.0 g Total Fat (1.3 g Mono, 0.8 g Poly, 0.5 g Sat); 8 mg Cholesterol; 54 g Carbohydrate; 17 g Fibre; 20 g Protein; 695 mg Sodium

Pictured below.

There's nothing like a comforting bowl of chicken noodle soup to cure what ails you! This long-simmered, made-from-scratch soup is well worth the effort. Use whichever cuts of chicken you prefer, as long as the weight used is equal to that listed.

make ahead

Freeze homemade stock in differently sized containers to flavour not just soups but gravies, sauces, risottos and other dishes. For very small amounts, freeze stock in ice cube trays or muffin tins, then transfer the cubes to a plastic freezer bag. No time to make your own stock? See page 6 for information on stock alternatives.

tip

To make stocks virtually fat-free, chill overnight and remove the solidified fat from the surface.

Comfort Chicken Noodle Soup   *A Classic!*

CHICKEN STOCK		
Bone-in chicken parts	4 lbs.	1.8 kg
Water	10 cups	2.5 L
Celery ribs, with leaves, halved	2	2
Large onion, quartered	1	1
Large carrot, halved	1	1
Sprigs of fresh thyme	3	3
Sprig of fresh parsley	1	1
Bay leaves	2	2
Garlic clove	1	1
Whole black peppercorns	12	12
SOUP		
Cooking oil	2 tsp.	10 mL
Chopped onion	1/2 cup	125 mL
Chopped carrot	1/2 cup	125 mL
Chopped celery	1/2 cup	125 mL
Spaghetti, broken into about 3 inch (7.5 cm) pieces	3 oz.	85 g
Chopped fresh parsley	1/4 cup	60 mL
Salt	3/4 tsp.	4 mL
Pepper	1/4 tsp.	1 mL

Chicken Stock: Put chicken and water into Dutch oven or large pot. Bring to a boil. Boil, uncovered, for 5 minutes without stirring. Skim and discard foam from side of pot.

Add next 8 ingredients. Stir. Bring to a boil. Reduce heat to medium-low. Simmer, uncovered, for about 3 hours, stirring occasionally, until chicken is tender and starts to fall off bones. Remove from heat. Remove chicken and bones to cutting board using slotted spoon. Remove chicken from bones. Discard bones and skin. Chop enough chicken to make 2 cups (500 mL). Reserve remaining chicken for another use. Strain stock through sieve into large bowl. Discard solids. Skim fat from stock. Makes about 6 1/2 cups (1.6 L) stock.

(continued on next page)

Soup: Heat cooking oil in large saucepan on medium. Add next 3 ingredients. Cook for 5 to 10 minutes, stirring often, until onion is softened. Add stock. Bring to a boil.

Add spaghetti. Cook, uncovered, for about 10 minutes, stirring occasionally, until spaghetti and vegetables are tender.

Add chicken and remaining 3 ingredients. Heat and stir until chicken is heated through. Makes about 7 1/2 cups (1.9 L).

1 cup (250 mL): 137 Calories; 4.3 g Total Fat (1.8 g Mono, 1.1 g Poly, 0.9 g Sat); 34 mg Cholesterol; 11 g Carbohydrate; 1 g Fibre; 13 g Protein; 287 mg Sodium

Pictured below.

A hearty chicken soup that's on the table in half an hour! A standard in any cook's repertoire.

serving suggestion

Serve with grilled cheese sandwiches made with sharp Cheddar cheese and whole-grain bread.

Chicken Pasta Soup

Cooking oil	1 tsp.	5 mL
Finely chopped onion	1 cup	250 mL
Lean ground chicken	1/2 lb.	225 g
Finely chopped celery	1/4 cup	60 mL
Precooked bacon slices, diced	4	4
Water	5 cups	1.25 L
Chicken bouillon powder	1 tbsp.	15 mL
Pepper	1/4 tsp.	1 mL
Frozen mixed vegetables	1 cup	250 mL
Tiny shell (or other very small) pasta	1/2 cup	125 mL
Parsley flakes (or 4 tsp., 20 mL, chopped fresh parsley)	1 tsp.	5 mL

Heat cooking oil in large frying pan on medium-high. Add next 4 ingredients. Scramble-fry for 5 to 10 minutes, stirring occasionally, until ground chicken is no longer pink and onion is softened. Drain.

Combine next 3 ingredients in large saucepan. Bring to a boil on medium-high.

Add chicken mixture, mixed vegetables and pasta. Stir. Cover. Bring to a boil. Reduce heat to medium-low. Simmer for about 10 minutes, stirring occasionally, until pasta is tender but firm.

Add parsley. Stir. Makes about 7 cups (1.75 L).

1 cup (250 mL): 145 Calories; 7.3 g Total Fat (1.4 g Mono, 0.6 g Poly, 0.8 g Sat); 3 mg Cholesterol; 11 g Carbohydrate; 1 g Fibre; 9 g Protein; 375 mg Sodium

Your standard chicken soup just went south of the border and came back with the exciting flavours of chipotle, lime and cilantro.

Chicken Corn Soup

Canola oil	1 tsp.	5 mL
Frozen kernel corn	2 cups	500 mL
Chopped onion	1 cup	250 mL
Garlic cloves, minced (or 1/2 tsp., 2 mL, powder)	2	2
Finely chopped chipotle pepper in adobo sauce (see Tip, right)	1/2 tsp.	2 mL

(continued on next page)

Low-sodium prepared chicken broth	3 cups	750 mL
Can of diced tomatoes (with juice)	14 oz.	398 mL
Pepper	1/4 tsp.	1 mL
Chopped cooked chicken (see Tip, page 36)	2 cups	500 mL
Chopped fresh cilantro	1 tbsp.	15 mL
Lime juice	1 tbsp.	15 mL

Heat canola oil in large saucepan on medium-high. Add next 4 ingredients. Cook, uncovered, for about 4 minutes, stirring often, until onion is softened.

Add next 3 ingredients. Stir. Bring to a boil. Reduce heat to medium. Boil gently, covered, for 6 minutes to blend flavours.

Add chicken. Cook and stir for about 3 minutes until heated through.

Add cilantro and lime juice. Stir. Makes about 7 cups (1.75 L). Serves 6.

1 serving: 201 Calories; 5.6 g Total Fat (1.8 g Mono, 1.1 g Poly, 1.1 g Sat); 58 mg Cholesterol; 16 g Carbohydrate; 1 g Fibre; 22 g Protein; 699 mg Sodium

Pictured below.

Chicken Corn Soup, left

about adobo sauce

Adobo is a thick, dark red Mexican sauce made of chilies, vinegar, herbs and spices. It's used as a marinade, sauce or as a condiment together with chipotle peppers.

tip

Chipotle chili peppers are smoked jalapeño peppers. Be sure to wash your hands after handling. Store leftover chipotle chili peppers with sauce in airtight container in refrigerator for up to 1 year.

Back bacon adds rich, smoky flavour to this light and colourful soup.

Make it a meal by adding a green salad and crusty bread.

Chicken and Bacon Pea Soup

Cooking oil	2 tsp.	10 mL
Chopped red pepper	1 cup	250 mL
Chopped green onion	1 cup	250 mL
Boneless, skinless chicken thighs, cut into 1/2 inch (12 mm) pieces	6 oz.	170 g
Chopped lean back bacon	1/3 cup	75 mL
Paprika	1/2 tsp.	2 mL
Pepper	1/2 tsp.	2 mL
All-purpose flour	2 tbsp.	30 mL
Milk	2 cups	500 mL
Low-sodium prepared chicken broth	2 cups	500 mL
Frozen peas	1 cup	250 mL
Light sour cream	2 tbsp.	30 mL

Heat cooking oil in large saucepan on medium. Add next 6 ingredients. Cook for 5 to 10 minutes, stirring occasionally, until chicken is no longer pink inside.

Add flour. Heat and stir for 1 minute.

Slowly add milk and broth, stirring constantly. Heat and stir until boiling and thickened. Reduce heat to medium-low. Simmer, uncovered, for 10 minutes, stirring occasionally.

Add peas and sour cream. Stir. Cover. Simmer for about 5 minutes, stirring occasionally, until peas are heated through. Makes 5 1/2 cups (1.4 L). Serves 6.

1 serving: 149 Calories; 5 g Total Fat (2.1 g Mono, 1.0 g Poly, 1.7 g Sat); 33 mg Cholesterol; 13 g Carbohydrate; 2 g Fibre; 13 g Protein; 361 mg Sodium

Pictured at right.

It's not a lie—everything but the chicken is blended smooth! This creamy, golden soup has a wonderful medley of vegetable and chicken flavours.

Only Chicken Soup

Chopped onion	1 cup	250 mL
Chopped celery	1 cup	250 mL
Garlic clove, minced (or 1/4 tsp., 1 mL, powder)	1	1
Cooking oil	1 tbsp.	15 mL

(continued on next page)

Water	6 cups	1.5 L
Chopped carrot (about 2 medium)	1 cup	250 mL
Medium potatoes, peeled and cut into 8 chunks	2	2
Peeled diced zucchini	1 1/2 cups	375 mL
Boneless, skinless chicken breast halves (about 2)	8 oz.	225 g
Chicken bouillon powder	3 tbsp.	50 mL
Parsley flakes	2 tsp.	10 mL
Bay leaf	1	1
Alphabet pasta, uncooked (optional)	1/2 cup	125 mL

Sauté onion, celery and garlic in cooking oil in large uncovered pot or Dutch oven until onion is soft and clear.

Stir in remaining 9 ingredients. Cover. Simmer for 1 hour. Remove chicken to cutting board. Remove and discard bay leaf. Purée soup, in 2 batches, in blender or with hand blender until smooth (see Safety Tip). Return to pot. Cut chicken into bite-sized pieces. Return to soup. Makes 10 2/3 cups (2.7 L).

1 cup (250 mL): 77 Calories; 1.9 g Total Fat (0.9 g Mono, 0.5 g Poly, 0.2 g Sat); 13 mg Cholesterol; 10 g Carbohydrate; 1 g Fibre; 6 g Protein; 961 mg Sodium

Pictured below.

Safety Tip: Follow manufacturer's instructions for processing hot liquids.

freezing

If you want to freeze Only Chicken Soup or any other containing pasta or potatoes, keep in mind that those ingredients do not freeze well, so you may want to consider adding them after thawing. Rice will soften after thawing; undercooking it slightly before freezing will prevent this from happening.

Left: Chicken and Bacon Pea Soup, left
Right: Only Chicken Soup, left

This filling Chinese-inspired soup has lots of corn, ham, chicken and cooked egg threads. A hint of sherry complements the flavours nicely.

about slurry

A slurry is a mixture of cold liquid and flour or cornstarch that is useful for thickening soup and other dishes. It's usually added slowly to hot ingredients and then cooked gently until boiling and thickened to eliminate any raw taste from the flour or cornstarch.

Sweet Corn Chicken Soup

Water	3 cups	750 mL
Can of cream-style corn	14 oz.	398 mL
Slice of deli ham, diced	1	1
Boneless, skinless chicken breast halves (about 2), cooked and chopped	1/2 lb.	225 g
Soy sauce	1/2 tsp.	2 mL
Chicken bouillon powder	1 tbsp.	15 mL
Chopped fresh chives	2 tsp.	10 mL
Salt	1/8 tsp.	0.5 mL
Pepper	1/8 tsp.	0.5 mL
Water	2 tbsp.	30 mL
Cornstarch	1 tbsp.	15 mL
Sherry (optional)	1 tbsp.	15 mL
Large egg, fork-beaten	1	1

Combine first 9 ingredients in large saucepan. Heat and stir until boiling.

Stir second amount of water into cornstarch in small cup until smooth. Stir into chicken mixture until boiling and thickened.

Add sherry. Stir. Add egg in a very fine stream, stirring constantly. Makes 5 1/4 cups (1.3 L).

1 cup (250 mL): 136 Calories; 2.0 g Total Fat (0.6 g Mono, 0.3 g Poly, 0.5 g Sat); 68 mg Cholesterol; 15 g Carbohydrate; 1 g Fibre; 13 g Protein; 1080 mg Sodium

A thick, attractively sage-coloured soup complete with generous amounts of chicken and the freshness of broccoli.

Broccoli Chicken Chowder

Packages of frozen cut broccoli (10 oz., 300 g, each)	2	2
Water	1 cup	250 mL
Milk	1 cup	250 mL
Can of skim evaporated milk	13 1/2 oz.	385 mL
Cans of condensed cream of chicken soup (10 oz., 284 mL, each)	2	2
Chicken bouillon powder	1 tbsp.	15 mL
Ground oregano	1/2 tsp.	2 mL

(continued on next page)

| Boneless, skinless chicken breast halves (about 2), diced | 1/2 lb. | 225 g |
| Hard margarine (or butter) | 1 tbsp. | 15 mL |

Cook broccoli in water in large saucepan until tender. Do not drain. Purée broccoli with liquid in blender (see Safety Tip). Return to saucepan.

Add both milks, chicken soup, bouillon powder and oregano. Stir.

Sauté chicken in margarine in frying pan until tender and no longer pink inside. Add to broccoli mixture. Simmer for about 5 minutes, stirring occasionally. Makes 9 cups (2.25 L).

1 cup (250 mL): 167 Calories; 6.2 g Total Fat (1.6 g Mono, 1.4 g Poly, 2.1 g Sat); 24 mg Cholesterol; 15 g Carbohydrate; 2 g Fibre; 13 g Protein; 966 mg Sodium

Safety Tip: Follow manufacturer's instructions for processing hot liquids.

Cock-a-Leekie Soup

A Classic!

Chicken Stock (page 26), or prepared chicken broth	10 cups	2.25 L
Leeks, white part only, chopped	8	8
Long-grain rice, uncooked	1/4 cup	60 mL
Quartered pitted dried prunes	1 1/2 cups	375 mL
Parsley flakes	1/2 tsp.	2 mL
Ground thyme	1/8 tsp.	0.5 mL
Salt	1/2 tsp.	2 mL
Pepper	1/4 tsp.	1 mL
Diced cooked chicken (see Tip, page 36)	3 cups	750 mL

Combine first 8 ingredients in large pot. Bring to a boil. Cook slowly for about 30 minutes.

Add chicken. Cover. Cook for another 10 minutes. Makes about 14 cups (3.2 L).

1 cup (250 mL): 125 Calories; 2.4 g Total Fat (0.9 g Mono, 0.5 g Poly, 0.7 g Sat); 27 mg Cholesterol; 15 g Carbohydrate; 1 g Fibre; 10 g Protein; 935 mg Sodium

A chicken and leek soup that was served in Scotland as early as the 16th century—it's sure to bring out the Scot in anyone! This version includes the traditional ingredient of dried prunes, which adds a rich flavour.

time-saving tip

If you've no time to make stock from scratch, make a quick substitute by using 10 cups (2.5 L) water plus 3 1/2 tbsp. (57 mL) chicken bouillon powder, or substitute an equal amount of store-bought chicken broth.

This is a full-bodied gumbo thickened with rice and vegetables. The okra gives it an authentic Southern feel!

about gumbo

Perhaps one of the most famous dishes to have come out of the United States, gumbo originated in Louisiana, but the word itself is thought to be derived from an African word for okra. Gumbo can contain many different kinds of vegetables, meats and shellfish, but all gumbos are thickened either with okra or a roux. In the southern U.S., fresh okra is the preferred thickener, and it's available year-round. Elsewhere it is in season from about May to October.

Plan for two days to create this rich and flavourful turkey soup—one day to boil, strain and chill the broth, and the next day to finish the soup.

about celery hearts

The celery heart is the very centre of a celery bunch, the inner ribs so to speak, including the small, pale-coloured stalks with leaves. Celery hearts are available in ready-to-use packages from the produce section in grocery stores.

Chicken Gumbo

Chicken Stock (page 26), or prepared chicken broth	8 cups	2 L
Chopped onion	1 cup	250 mL
Canned tomatoes, broken up	14 oz.	398 mL
Sliced okra	1 cup	250 mL
Small green pepper, seeded and chopped	1	1
Finely chopped celery	1/4 cup	60 mL
Long-grain rice, uncooked	1/2 cup	125 mL
Granulated sugar	1 tsp.	5 mL
Salt	1 tsp.	5 mL
Pepper	1/4 tsp.	1 mL
Diced cooked chicken (see Tip, page 36)	2 cups	500 mL

Put first 10 ingredients into large pot. Cover. Bring to a boil, stirring often. Boil gently for about 20 minutes until rice is cooked.

Add chicken. Cook until heated through. Makes about 10 cups (2.5 L).

1 cup (250 mL): 134 Calories; 3.3 g Total Fat (1.2 g Mono, 0.7 g Poly, 0.9 g Sat); 25 mg Cholesterol; 12 g Carbohydrate; 1 g Fibre; 13 g Protein; 932 mg Sodium

Meaty Turkey Rice Soup

DAY 1		
Water	12 cups	3 L
Turkey parts, with skin	6 lbs.	2.7 kg
Whole celery heart	1	1
Medium onions, halved	2	2
Large carrot, halved	1	1
Bay leaves	2	2
Peppercorns	10	10
Fresh parsley sprigs	2	2
Salt	1 tbsp.	15 mL
DAY 2		
Water		
Chopped onion	1 cup	250 mL
Chopped celery	1 cup	250 mL
Diced carrot	1 cup	250 mL

(continued on next page)

Reserved cooked turkey	4 cups	1 L
Cooked long-grain white rice	1 1/2 cups	375 mL
(about 1/2 cup, 125 mL, uncooked)		
Frozen peas	1 cup	250 mL
Chopped fresh parsley	1/4 cup	60 mL
(or 1 tbsp., 15 mL, flakes)		
Salt, to taste		
Pepper, to taste		

Day 1: Combine water and turkey parts in at least 6 quart (6 L) Dutch oven or stockpot. Bring to a boil. Boil, uncovered, for 5 minutes. Remove from heat. Carefully spoon off and discard foam from surface. Bring to a boil.

Add next 7 ingredients. Reduce heat. Simmer, partially covered, for about 3 hours until meat is falling off bones. Pour through sieve over large liquid measure. Remove meat from turkey bones as soon as cool enough to handle. Dice meat. Reserve 4 cups (1 L). Cover. Chill. Discard skin, turkey bones and strained solids. Chill broth overnight until fat comes to surface and solidifies.

Day 2: Carefully spoon off and discard fat from surface of broth. Add water, if necessary, to make 10 cups (2.5 L). Pour into Dutch oven or stockpot. Bring to a boil. Add onion, celery and carrot. Reduce heat. Simmer, partially covered, for 1 hour.

Add remaining 6 ingredients. Cook gently for about 10 minutes until heated through. Makes about 10 1/2 cups (2.6 L).

1 cup (250 mL): 147 Calories; 2.9 g Total Fat (0.6 g Mono, 0.8 g Poly, 0.9 g Sat); 41 mg Cholesterol; 12 g Carbohydrate; 2 g Fibre; 18 g Protein; 745 mg Sodium

Pictured below.

tip

If you're watching your weight, soup can make a nutritious, filling meal. To reduce calories even further, trim the fat off any meat you use, or drain it away if you're searing it first. You can further reduce the fat of broth-based soups by placing a coffee filter on the soup's surface and blotting it up. Or, if you let the soup chill in the refrigerator overnight, the fat will harden on the surface, making it easy to lift out.

Meaty Turkey Rice Soup, left

Who says chicken soup has the cure-all market cornered? This slow-cooker turkey soup is so comforting, and has just the right blend of spicy and sour ingredients, to perk you up in no time.

tip

Don't have any leftover chicken or turkey? Start with 2 boneless, skinless chicken breasts (4 – 6 oz., 113 – 117 g, each) or 1 boneless, skinless turkey breast (about 10 oz., 285 g). Place in large frying pan with 1 cup (250 mL) water or chicken broth. Simmer, covered, for 12 to 14 minutes until no longer pink inside. Drain. Chop. Makes about 2 cups (500 mL).

Hot and Sour Turkey Pot Soup

Chinese dried mushrooms	6	6
Boiling water	1 cup	250 mL
Prepared chicken broth	4 cups	1 L
Diced cooked turkey (see Tip, left)	2 cups	500 mL
Sliced carrot	2 cups	500 mL
Cubed firm tofu	1 cup	250 mL
Sliced celery	1 cup	250 mL
Soy sauce	1/4 cup	60 mL
Rice vinegar	2 tbsp.	30 mL
Chili paste (sambal oelek)	1 tsp.	5 mL
Prepared chicken broth	1/4 cup	60 mL
Cornstarch	2 tbsp.	30 mL
Sesame oil (optional)	1 tsp.	5 mL
Chopped baby bok choy	2 cups	500 mL
Thinly sliced green onion	1/4 cup	60 mL
Rice vinegar	1 tbsp.	15 mL

Put mushrooms into small heatproof bowl. Add boiling water. Stir. Let stand for about 20 minutes until softened. Drain. Remove and discard stems. Slice into thin strips. Transfer to 3 1/2 to 4 quart (3.5 to 4 L) slow cooker.

Add next 8 ingredients. Stir well. Cook, covered, on Low for 4 to 6 hours or High for 2 to 3 hours until carrot is tender.

Combine next 3 ingredients in small bowl. Add to slow cooker. Stir.

Add bok choy and green onion. Stir well. Cook, covered, on High for about 5 minutes until slightly thickened.

Stir in second amount of vinegar. Makes about 8 cups (2 L).

1 cup (250 mL): 118 Calories; 2.1 g Total Fat (0.6 g Mono, 0.6 g Poly, 0.6 g Sat); 34 mg Cholesterol; 9 g Carbohydrate; 2 g Fibre; 15 g Protein; 1142 mg Sodium

Pictured at right and on back cover.

This delectable chowder is thick and almost stew-like. For an extra-special occasion, add shrimp, scallops or lobster.

make ahead

This hearty chowder is easy to make ahead and freeze in air-tight containers.

Clam Chowder

Large potatoes, cubed	3	3
Large carrots, cut into 1 inch (2.5 cm) pieces	3	3
Boiling water, to cover		
Bacon slices, diced	10 –12	10 –12
Large green pepper, diced	1	1
Chopped celery	1 1/2 cups	375 mL
Chopped onion	1 1/2 cups	375 mL
Reserved clam liquid		
Cans of condensed cream of potato soup (10 oz., 284 mL, each)	2	2
Lemon pepper	1/4 tsp.	1 mL
Salt	1 tsp.	5 mL
Pepper	1/8 tsp.	0.5 mL
Cans of baby clams, drained, liquid reserved (5 oz., 142 g, each)	2	2
Canned stewed tomatoes	14 oz.	398 mL
Milk	1 1/2 cups	375 mL

(continued on next page)

Clam Chowder, above

Cook potato and carrot in boiling water in large saucepan until tender. Do not drain.

Fry bacon until crisp. Remove to dish. Discard fat except for 1 tbsp. (15 mL).

Add green pepper, celery and onion to frying pan. Sauté until soft. Add to potato mixture along with bits from pan. Add bacon.

Add liquid from clams, potato soup, lemon pepper, salt and pepper. Stir. Boil gently for 10 to 15 minutes.

Add clams, tomatoes and milk. Heat through, without boiling, to prevent curdling. Makes 20 cups (5 L) chowder.

1 cup (250 mL): 128 Calories; 3.4 g Total Fat (1.0 g Mono, 0.3 g Poly, 1.4 g Sat); 19 mg Cholesterol; 19 g Carbohydrate; 2 g Fibre; 6 g Protein; 546 mg Sodium

Pictured at left.

Tuna Corn Chowder

Hard margarine (or butter)	1 tbsp.	15 mL
Chopped onion	1/3 cup	75 mL
Chopped celery	1/4 cup	60 mL
Water	1 1/2 cups	375 mL
Diced peeled potato	1 cup	250 mL
Chicken bouillon powder	1 tsp.	5 mL
Dill weed	1/2 tsp.	2 mL
Salt	1/2 tsp.	2 mL
Pepper	1/4 tsp.	1 mL
Can of cream-style corn	14 oz.	398 mL
Milk	1 cup	250 mL
Can of flaked tuna, drained	6 oz.	170 g

A simple can of tuna turns corn chowder into a complete meal! A pleasantly creamy soup with a hint of dill.

make ahead

This recipe freezes well, so why not make a batch or two on the weekend and freeze it in dinner-sized portions for quick weeknight meals? Use airtight containers to reduce freezer burn.

Melt margarine in large saucepan on medium. Add onion and celery. Cook for 5 to 10 minutes, stirring often, until onion is softened.

Add next 6 ingredients. Stir. Bring to a boil on medium-high. Reduce heat to medium-low. Cover. Simmer for about 10 minutes until potato is tender.

Add corn, milk and tuna. Heat for about 10 minutes, stirring occasionally, until heated through. Do not boil. Makes about 5 cups (1.25 L).

1 cup (250 mL): 176 Calories; 4.3 g Total Fat (2.1 g Mono, 0.8 g Poly, 1.2 g Sat); 15 mg Cholesterol; 25 g Carbohydrate; 2 g Fibre; 11 g Protein; 787 mg Sodium

Traditionally served with a pat of butter or swirls of whipping cream, this Scottish smoked fish soup makes a great cold-day supper.

about cullen skink

This soup is named for the town of Cullen in Morayshire, Scotland. "Skink" is a Scottish word meaning "beef shank," but the term is also used more generally to mean "soup."

variation

If smoked haddock is hard to find, substitute smoked cod.

This Thai-influenced soup has a wonderful combination of curry spice and herb freshness. Adjust the amount of green curry paste to suit your heat preference.

make ahead

Curries often improve in flavour if the spices are left to mellow for a day, so you may find that your curry soup actually tastes better the next day.

Cullen Skink

Finnan haddie (smoked haddock)	1 lb.	454 g
Medium onion, chopped	1	1
Water	3 cups	750 mL
Mashed potatoes	2 1/2 cups	625 mL
Skim evaporated milk	2/3 cup	150 mL
Milk	1 3/4 cups	425 mL
Chopped fresh parsley (or 1 tsp., 5 mL, flakes)	1 1/2 tbsp.	25 mL
Pepper	1/8 tsp.	0.5 mL

Cook fish and onion in water in large saucepan for 20 minutes. Do not drain. Remove fish. Remove bones, flaking flesh from skin. Return fish to saucepan.

Add remaining 5 ingredients. Stir well. Bring to a boil, stirring frequently. Makes 8 cups (2 L).

1 cup (250 mL): 175 Calories; 2.0 g Total Fat (0.6 g Mono, 0.4 g Poly, 0.8 g Sat); 48 mg Cholesterol; 19 g Carbohydrate; trace Fibre; 20 g Protein; 660 mg Sodium

Coconut Shrimp Soup

Finely grated ginger root (or 1/2 tsp., 2 mL, ground ginger)	2 tsp.	10 mL
Garlic cloves, minced (or 1/2 tsp., 2 mL, powder)	2	2
Green curry paste	1 tbsp.	15 mL
Cooking oil	2 tsp.	10 mL
Cans of light coconut milk (14 oz., 398 mL, each)	2	2
Prepared chicken broth	1 cup	250 mL
Stalk of lemon grass, halved	1	1
Fish sauce	2 tsp.	10 mL
Brown sugar, packed	2 tsp.	10 mL
Fresh snow peas, trimmed, thinly sliced lengthwise	4 oz.	113 g

(continued on next page)

Raw medium shrimp, peeled and deveined	1 lb.	454 g
Chopped fresh basil	3 tbsp.	50 mL
(or 2 1/4 tsp., 11 mL, dried)		
Chopped fresh cilantro (or parsley)	3 tbsp.	50 mL

Sauté ginger, garlic and curry paste in cooking oil in large saucepan for 1 to 2 minutes until fragrant.

Add next 6 ingredients. Stir. Bring to a boil on medium-high. Cover. Reduce heat to medium. Simmer for 2 minutes to blend flavours.

Add remaining 3 ingredients. Reduce heat to medium-low. Heat and stir for 3 to 5 minutes until shrimp are just pink. Remove and discard lemon grass. Makes 6 cups (1.5 L).

1 cup (250 mL): 255 Calories; 16.2 g Total Fat (1.2 g Mono, 1.1 g Poly, 12.9 g Sat); 115 mg Cholesterol; 8 g Carbohydrate; 1 g Fibre; 18 g Protein; 476 mg Sodium

Pictured below.

about green curry

Curries are a major part of Thai cuisine, and they're often named by their colour—yellow, red and green. Yellow is the mildest and green is the hottest. Green curry paste and green curries get their colour from the green chilies used to make them.

Coconut Shrimp Soup, left

This deliciously simple and elegant soup is creamy white with mild and delicate flavours.

time-saving tip

When making this soup, try mixing just 1 cup (250 mL) of the milk with the flour, bouillon powder and pepper, and let this come to a boil before adding the remaining 3 cups (750 mL) of milk. The milk will boil much faster this way than if you try boiling all 4 cups (1 L) at once.

A lovely soup with plenty of leafy spinach and sweet shrimp. The rich broth, perfectly accented with white wine, makes this soup a special treat.

Simple Crab Soup

Butter (or hard margarine)	1/3 cup	75 mL
All-purpose flour	1/3 cup	75 mL
Chicken bouillon powder	1 tbsp.	15 mL
Pepper (white is best for colour)	1/8 tsp.	0.5 mL
Milk	4 cups	1 L
Crabmeat (or 4 1/4 oz., 120 g, can, drained, cartilage removed)	1 cup	250 mL
Sherry	1 1/2 tbsp.	25 mL

Chopped chives, for garnish

Melt butter in saucepan. Mix in flour, bouillon powder and pepper. Stir in milk until it boils and thickens.

Add crabmeat and sherry. Heat through but do not boil.

Sprinkle each serving with chives. Makes 5 cups (1.25 L).

1 cup (250 mL): 255 Calories; 14.6 g Total Fat (4.1 g Mono, 0.6 g Poly, 9.0 g Sat); 66 mg Cholesterol; 18 g Carbohydrate; trace Fibre; 13 g Protein; 956 mg Sodium

Spinach and Shrimp Soup

Uncooked medium shrimp (with shells)	1 lb.	454 g
Water	7 cups	1.75 L
Dry white (or alcohol-free) wine	1 cup	250 mL
Chopped onion	1/2 cup	125 mL
Chopped carrot	1/2 cup	125 mL
Olive (or canola) oil	1 tbsp.	15 mL
Chopped onion	1 cup	250 mL
Garlic cloves, minced (or 1 tsp., 5 mL, powder)	4	4
All-purpose flour	1 tbsp.	15 mL
Fresh spinach, stems removed, coarsely chopped, lightly packed	6 cups	1.5 L
Chopped fresh parsley (or 1 1/2 tsp., 7 mL, flakes)	2 tbsp.	30 mL
Salt	1 tsp.	5 mL
Can of evaporated milk	5 1/2 oz.	160 mL

(continued on next page)

Peel and devein shrimp, reserving shells and tails. Coarsely chop shrimp. Transfer to medium bowl. Set aside.

Put reserved shells and tails into large pot or Dutch oven. Add next 4 ingredients. Stir. Bring to a boil on medium-high. Reduce heat to medium. Simmer, uncovered, for 20 minutes, stirring occasionally. Strain through sieve into large bowl. Discard solids. Set liquid aside.

Heat olive oil in same pot on medium. Add second amount of onion. Cook for 5 to 10 minutes, stirring often, until softened.

Add garlic. Heat and stir for 1 to 2 minutes until fragrant.

Add flour. Heat and stir for 1 minute. Slowly add reserved liquid, stirring constantly until boiling and slightly thickened. Reduce heat to medium-low. Simmer, uncovered, for 5 minutes, stirring occasionally.

Add spinach, parsley and salt. Heat and stir for about 3 minutes until spinach is wilted.

Add shrimp and evaporated milk. Heat and stir on medium-high for about 2 minutes until shrimp turn pink. Makes about 8 cups (2 L) soup. Serves 6.

1 serving: 202 Calories; 6.1 g Total Fat (2.6 g Mono, 0.9 g Poly, 2.0 g Sat); 110 mg Cholesterol; 12 g Carbohydrate; 3 g Fibre; 18 g Protein; 581 mg Sodium

Pictured below.   Spinach and Shrimp Soup, left

Though people often expect shellfish to be the base ingredient in bisques, this version uses basa instead. We've also used evaporated milk as a lower-fat alternative to the traditional cream.

about bisque

On the soup family tree, bisque is a close relative of chowder. Both are rich, thick soups often made with a seafood base, the main difference being that chowders are chunky while bisques are smooth. Several hundred years ago, the term "bisque" was used to describe a spicy dish of meat or game birds. By the 1700s, crayfish became the dominant ingredient, and from that point on bisque became known mainly as a seafood-based soup, although bisques can also feature meat or vegetables as a main ingredient.

Basa Bisque

Cooking oil	1 tsp.	5 mL
Chopped onion	1 cup	250 mL
Chopped celery	1/2 cup	125 mL
Garlic cloves, minced (or 1/2 tsp., 2 mL, powder)	2	2
Water	2 1/2 cups	625 mL
Chopped peeled potatoes	2 cups	500 mL
Can of cut yellow wax beans (with liquid)	14 oz.	398 mL
Chopped carrot	1 cup	250 mL
Frozen kernel corn	1/2 cup	125 mL
Bay leaf	1	1
Can of evaporated milk	13 1/2 oz.	385 mL
Milk	1 cup	250 mL
All-purpose flour	1/4 cup	60 mL
Salt	1 1/2 tsp.	7 mL
Pepper	1/2 tsp.	2 mL
Ground nutmeg	1/8 tsp.	0.5 mL
Basa fillets, any small bones removed, cut into 1 inch (2.5 cm) pieces	1 lb.	454 g

Heat cooking oil in Dutch oven on medium. Add next 3 ingredients. Cook for 5 to 10 minutes, stirring often, until onion is softened.

Add next 6 ingredients. Stir. Bring to a boil. Reduce heat to medium-low. Simmer, covered, for about 20 minutes, stirring occasionally, until vegetables are soft.

Whisk next 6 ingredients in small bowl until smooth. Add to vegetables. Stir well on medium until boiling and thickened slightly.

Add fish. Simmer for 5 minutes, stirring occasionally, until fish flakes easily when tested with fork. Remove and discard bay leaf. Carefully process, in 3 batches, in blender (see Safety Tip). Makes about 9 1/4 cups (2.3 L).

1 cup (250 mL): 194 Calories; 5.6 g Total Fat (1.0 g Mono, 0.3 g Poly, 3.0 g Sat); 37 mg Cholesterol; 24 g Carbohydrate; 3 g Fibre; 12 g Protein; 705 mg Sodium

Pictured at right.

Safety Tip: Follow manufacturer's instructions for processing hot liquids

Simple Seafood Bisque

Can of ready-to-serve New England clam chowder	19 oz.	540 mL
Can of condensed tomato soup	10 oz.	284 mL
Can of crabmeat, drained, cartilage removed, flaked	6 oz.	170 g
Water	1 cup	250 mL
Medium sherry	2 tbsp.	30 mL

Process chowder in blender or food processor until smooth. Transfer to medium saucepan.

Add soup. Stir. Add crabmeat and water. Stir well. Heat on medium-low, stirring often, until boiling. Remove from heat.

Add sherry. Stir. Makes about 4 3/4 cups (1.2 L).

1 cup (250 mL): 148 Calories; 4.4 g Total Fat (1.3 g Mono, 1.0 g Poly, 1.6 g Sat); 11 mg Cholesterol; 17 g Carbohydrate; 1 g Fibre; 10 g Protein; 1130 mg Sodium

Pictured below.

Sherry provides a subtle sweetness to this creamy combination of just a few simple ingredients. Garnish with green onion to add a special touch

Left: Simple Seafood Bisque, above
Right: Basa Bisque, left

A chunky crab soup with colourful tomatoes and vegetables—so tasty!

variation

Turn Crab Soup into tuna soup by using canned tuna with liquid instead of crabmeat.

Crab Soup

Canned stewed tomatoes	14 oz.	398 mL
Chopped onion	1 cup	250 mL
Chopped celery	1/2 cup	125 mL
Grated potato	1 1/2 cups	375 mL
Grated carrot	1/2 cup	125 mL
Water	3 cups	750 mL
Milk	1/2 cup	125 mL
All-purpose flour	1/4 cup	60 mL
Chicken bouillon powder	1 tbsp.	15 mL
Salt	1 tsp.	5 mL
Pepper	1/8 – 1/4 tsp.	0.5 – 1 mL
Can of evaporated skim milk (or light cream)	13 1/2 oz.	385 mL
Can of crabmeat, with liquid, cartilage removed	4 1/4 oz.	120 g

Combine first 6 ingredients in saucepan. Cover. Cook until vegetables are tender.

Measure next 5 ingredients into small bowl. Whisk until no lumps remain. Stir into tomato mixture until it boils and thickens.

Add evaporated milk and crabmeat. Heat slowly, stirring often, until steaming hot, but not boiling. Makes 8 cups (2 L).

1 cup (250 mL): 119 Calories; 0.5 g Total Fat (0.1 g Mono, 0.1 g Poly, 0.2 g Sat); 13 mg Cholesterol; 21 g Carbohydrate; 1 g Fibre; 8 g Protein; 940 mg Sodium

Pictured at right.

This traditional gumbo will have you feeling like you're down on the bayou. Full of rice, vegetables and seafood, it will satisfy any appetite.

serving suggestion

Serve with a bottle of hot sauce for those who want to up the spice factor!

Seafood Gumbo

Cooking oil	1 tbsp.	15 mL
Chopped celery	1 cup	250 mL
Chopped onion	1 cup	250 mL
Cajun seasoning	1 1/2 tsp.	7 mL
Garlic clove, minced (or 1/4 tsp., 1 mL, powder)	1	1
Dried thyme	1/4 tsp.	1 mL
Pepper	1/4 tsp.	1 mL

(continued on next page)

All-purpose flour	2 tbsp.	30 mL
Prepared vegetable broth	3 cups	750 mL
Can of diced tomatoes (with juice)	14 oz.	398 mL
Fresh (or frozen) okra, chopped (optional)	1 cup	250 mL
Long-grain white rice	1/2 cup	125 mL
Bay leaves	2	2
Cod fillets, any small bones removed, cut into 1 inch (2.5 cm) pieces	1 cup	250 mL
Frozen seafood mix, thawed	1 cup	250 mL

Heat cooking oil in large saucepan or Dutch oven on medium. Add next 6 ingredients. Cook for about 10 minutes, stirring occasionally, until onion is browned.

Add flour. Heat and stir for about 5 minutes until flour starts to turn brown. Slowly add broth, stirring constantly and scraping any brown bits from bottom of pan, until boiling and thickened.

Add next 4 ingredients. Stir. Bring to a boil. Cook, covered, for about 15 minutes until rice is almost tender. Remove and discard bay leaves.

Add fish and seafood mix. Stir. Cook, covered, for about 10 minutes until fish flakes easily when tested with fork and rice is tender. Makes about 6 cups (1.5 L).

1 cup (250 mL): 172 Calories; 3.1 g Total Fat (1.4 g Mono, 0.9 g Poly, 0.3 g Sat); 65 mg Cholesterol; 23 g Carbohydrate; 1 g Fibre; 14 g Protein; 667 mg Sodium

about roux

Gumbos often use a roux (ROO) as a thickener. To make a traditional roux, heat butter or other fat and stir in an equal amount of flour. Cook the flour in the fat for a few minutes until it starts to lightly brown. Once the roux is made, add liquid to it slowly while stirring and heat it to a boil. Make sure to stir continuously to prevent lumps from forming as you proceed with your recipe.

Crab Soup, left

This soup is a lightened-up version of cioppino (cho-PEE-no), a classic stew containing fish, seafood and often shell-on shellfish, in a broth of tomato and fish stock.

food fun

Cioppino is thought to have been invented by the Italian and Portuguese fishermen who immigrated to San Francisco in the 19th century. Credit for the name of the soup is given to the Italians, as it's said to come from the Genovese word *ciuppin,* meaning "to chop."

serving suggestion

Serve with a thick slice of fresh sourdough or garlic bread for a hearty and delicious lunch.

Tomato Seafood Soup   *A Classic!*

Olive (or cooking) oil	2 tbsp.	30 mL
Chopped fennel bulb (white part only)	1 cup	250 mL
Chopped onion	1 cup	250 mL
Garlic clove, minced (or 1/4 tsp., 1 mL, powder)	1	1
Dried crushed chilies	1/4 tsp.	1 mL
Dry (or alcohol-free) white wine	1/2 cup	125 mL
Clam tomato beverage	3 cups	750 mL
Prepared vegetable broth	3 cups	750 mL
Can of diced tomatoes (with juice)	14 oz.	398 mL
Bay leaf	1	1
Can of whole baby clams (with liquid)	5 oz.	142 g
Halibut fillet, any small bones removed, cut into 3/4 inch (2 cm) pieces	4 oz.	113 g
Small bay scallops	4 oz.	113 g
Uncooked medium shrimp (peeled and deveined)	4 oz.	113 g
Chopped fresh parsley	1 tbsp.	15 mL
Chopped fresh thyme	2 tsp.	10 mL

Heat olive oil in large saucepan or Dutch oven on medium. Add fennel and onion. Cook for about 10 minutes, stirring often, until onion is softened and starting to brown.

Add garlic and chilies. Heat and stir for 1 minute. Add wine. Simmer until liquid is reduced by half.

Add next 4 ingredients. Stir. Bring to a boil. Reduce heat to medium-low. Cook, partially covered, for 30 minutes to blend flavours. Remove and discard bay leaf.

Add remaining 6 ingredients. Stir. Cook for about 3 minutes, stirring frequently, until shrimp turn pink and scallops are opaque. Makes about 10 2/3 cups (2.7 L).

1 cup (250 mL): 134 Calories; 3.9 g Total Fat (2.0 g Mono, 0.6 g Poly, 0.6 g Sat); 34 mg Cholesterol; 14 g Carbohydrate; 1 g Fibre; 10 g Protein; 590 mg Sodium

Pictured at right.

A favourite variation of clam chowder, with a rich red-orange broth and wonderful flavours.

food fun

Just in case you can't keep them straight, Manhattan clam chowder is tomato-based while New England-style clam chowder is made with milk or cream. Manhattan-style is said to have been created by Portuguese immigrants and named after New York by New Englanders, who were scornful of what they thought was an inferior soup (and an inferior locale)! It's said that many restaurants will feature one chowder or the other on their menus, but not both types.

Manhattan Clam Chowder

Bacon slices, diced	4	4
Chopped onion	1 cup	250 mL
Medium potatoes, peeled and diced	2	2
Canned tomatoes, broken up	14 oz.	398 mL
Finely diced celery	1 cup	250 mL
Chicken bouillon powder	1 tbsp.	15 mL
Salt	1/2 tsp.	2 mL
Pepper	1/4 tsp.	1 mL
Ground thyme	1/4 tsp.	1 mL
Cayenne pepper (optional but good)	1/8 tsp.	0.5 mL
Water	3 cups	750 mL
All-purpose flour	1/4 cup	60 mL
Water	1 cup	250 mL
Can of baby clams, with liquid, chopped	5 oz.	142 g

Fry bacon and onion in Dutch oven until bacon is cooked and onion is clear.

Add next 9 ingredients. Bring to a boil. Boil gently, covered, for about 25 minutes until vegetables are tender.

Mix flour and second amount of water until smooth. Stir into boiling mixture until it returns to a boil and thickens.

Add clams and liquid. Heat through. Makes 7 1/3 cups (1.8 L).

1 cup (250 mL): 155 Calories; 6.4 g Total Fat (2.5 g Mono, 0.7 g Poly, 2.1 g Sat); 24 mg Cholesterol; 18 g Carbohydrate; 2 g Fibre; 7 g Protein; 1062 mg Sodium

Pictured at right.

This quick and easy soup covers all your bases with a good helping of broccoli, pasta and fish—great to serve for a light yet satisfying meal.

Broccoli and Haddock Soup

Prepared chicken broth	4 cups	1 L
Water	2 cups	500 mL
Garlic clove, minced	1	1
(or 1/4 tsp., 1 mL, powder)		
Tiny shell pasta	1 cup	250 mL
Chopped broccoli	2 cups	500 mL
Haddock fillets, any small bones removed, cut into bite-sized pieces	1 lb.	454 g
Lemon juice	1 tbsp.	15 mL
Salt	1/2 tsp.	2 mL
Pepper	1/2 tsp.	2 mL

Combine first 3 ingredients in large saucepan or Dutch oven. Bring to a boil. Add pasta. Reduce heat to medium. Boil gently, uncovered, for 8 minutes, stirring occasionally, until pasta is almost tender.

Add broccoli and fish. Cook for about 5 minutes until broccoli and pasta are tender.

Add remaining 3 ingredients. Stir. Makes about 8 cups (2 L).

1 cup (250 mL): 110 Calories; 1.2 g Total Fat (0.3 g Mono, 0.4 g Poly, 0.3 g Sat); 32 mg Cholesterol; 11 g Carbohydrate; 1 g Fibre; 13 g Protein; 931 mg Sodium

Sweet-and-sour soup gently accented with ginger—an enticing combination.

Pineapple Shrimp Soup

Uncooked medium shrimp (peeled and deveined)	1 lb.	454 g
Soy sauce	1 tbsp.	15 mL
Granulated sugar	1 tbsp.	15 mL
Garlic cloves, minced	2	2
(or 1/2 tsp., 2 mL, powder)		
Finely grated, peeled ginger root	1 tsp.	5 mL
(or 1/4 tsp., 1 mL, ground ginger)		
Pepper	1/2 tsp.	2 mL

(continued on next page)

Cooking oil	2 tsp.	10 mL
Medium onion, cut into 12 wedges	1	1
Prepared chicken broth	4 cups	1 L
Can of pineapple tidbits (with juice)	14 oz.	398 mL
Medium tomatoes, quartered, seeds removed, diced	2	2
Green onions, cut into 1 inch (2.5 cm) pieces	2	2
Finely shredded basil (or 1 tbsp., 15 mL, dried)	1/4 cup	60 mL
Chopped fresh cilantro or parsley	2 tbsp.	30 mL

Put first 6 ingredients into medium bowl. Stir gently until shrimp are coated. Heat wok or Dutch oven on medium-high. Add shrimp mixture. Stir-fry for 1 to 2 minutes until shrimp just start to turn pink. Transfer to medium bowl. Set aside.

Heat cooking oil in same wok. Add onion wedges. Stir-fry for about 2 minutes until starting to soften.

Add broth and pineapple with juice. Bring to a boil. Reduce heat to medium. Cover. Simmer for 5 minutes, stirring occasionally, to blend flavours.

Add remaining 4 ingredients. Heat and stir for about 5 minutes until heated through. Add shrimp mixture. Stir for about 1 minute until heated through. Makes about 8 cups (2 L).

1 cup (250 mL): 129 Calories; 2.8 g Total Fat (1.2 g Mono, 0.9 g Poly, 0.5 g Sat); 65 mg Cholesterol; 14 g Carbohydrate; 1 g Fibre; 12 g Protein; 608 mg Sodium

An egg drop-style soup with sophisticated flavours, this whips up quickly with easy-to-find ingredients.

about asparagus

Not only does asparagus have a great fresh flavour, but it's also very nutritious. It's high in vitamins A and C, protein, fibre, potassium and folate, low in calories and sodium and has no fat or cholesterol.

Crab Asparagus Soup

Cooking oil	1 tsp.	5 mL
Sliced fresh white mushrooms	1/2 cup	125 mL
Chopped green onion	1/4 cup	60 mL
Garlic clove, minced	1	1
(or 1/4 tsp., 1 mL, powder)		
Finely grated, peeled ginger root	1/4 tsp.	1 mL
Pepper	1/4 tsp.	1 mL
Prepared chicken broth	3 cups	750 mL
Fresh asparagus, trimmed of tough ends, cut into 1 inch (2.5 cm) pieces	1/2 lb.	225 g
Can of crabmeat, drained, cartilage removed, flaked	6 oz.	170 g
Cornstarch	2 tsp.	10 mL
Soy sauce	2 tsp.	10 mL
Hoisin sauce	2 tsp.	10 mL
Large egg	1	1
Water	1 tbsp.	15 mL

Heat cooking oil in medium saucepan on medium. Add next 5 ingredients. Cook for 5 to 10 minutes, stirring often, until onion is softened.

Add broth. Stir. Bring to a boil on medium-high.

Add asparagus and crabmeat. Cover. Reduce heat to medium. Boil gently for about 5 minutes until asparagus is tender-crisp.

Combine next 3 ingredients in small cup. Add to soup. Heat and stir for about 1 minute until boiling and slightly thickened.

Beat egg and water with fork in same small cup. Add to soup in thin stream, stirring constantly. Makes about 4 1/2 cups (1.1 L).

1 cup (250 mL): 119 Calories; 3.7 g Total Fat (1.5 g Mono, 0.9 g Poly, 0.8 g Sat); 79 mg Cholesterol; 8 g Carbohydrate; 1 g Fibre; 14 g Protein; 900 mg Sodium

Pictured at right.

This hot and spicy Thai specialty features ginger, lemon grass and lime. Reduce the amount of red chilies if you like it milder.

dinner themes

Tom Yum Soup features a classic Thai combination of robust salty, sour and hot flavours. For this reason, this soup would make a great starter for any Asian-themed dinner that features sweet or spicy curries.

Tom Yum Soup

Prepared chicken broth	4 cups	1 L
Thinly sliced fresh shiitake mushrooms	1 cup	250 mL
Ginger root slices (1/4 inch, 6 mm thick)	3	3
Lemon grass, bulbs only (roots and stalks removed)	3	3
Uncooked medium shrimp (peeled and deveined)	3/4 lb.	340 g
Can of shoestring-style bamboo shoots, drained	8 oz.	227 mL
Thai hot chili peppers, chopped (see Tip, page 15)	3	3
Lime juice	3 tbsp.	50 mL
Fish sauce	2 tbsp.	30 mL
Chopped fresh cilantro (or parsley)	2 tsp.	10 mL

Measure broth into large saucepan. Bring to a boil. Reduce heat to medium. Add mushrooms and ginger root. Simmer, uncovered, for about 5 minutes until mushrooms are tender.

Pound lemon grass bulbs with mallet or rolling pin until partially crushed. Add to broth mixture. Add next 3 ingredients. Stir. Simmer, uncovered, for about 2 minutes until shrimp turn pink. Remove from heat. Remove and discard ginger root and lemon grass.

Add remaining 3 ingredients. Stir. Makes about 5 cups (1.25 L). Serves 4.

1 serving: 151 Calories; 2.9 g Total Fat (0.6 g Mono, 1.1 g Poly, 0.6 g Sat); 129 mg Cholesterol; 10 g Carbohydrate; 2 g Fibre; 21 g Protein; 2302 mg Sodium

Pictured at right.

A satisfying soup filled with delicate wontons, tasty shrimp and fresh vegetables. This soup is best served immediately, before the wontons become too soft.

basic pork wontons

Lean ground pork	4 oz.	113 g
Cold water	1 tbsp.	15 mL
Finely chopped green onion	1 tbsp.	15 mL
Dry sherry	1 1/2 tsp.	6 mL
Cornstarch	3/4 tsp.	3 mL
Ground ginger	1/4 tsp.	1 mL
Salt	1/4 tsp.	1 mL
Pepper, sprinkle		
Wonton wrappers (keep covered with damp cloth)	20	20

Combine first 8 ingredients in medium bowl until well mixed.

Place about 1 tsp. (5 mL) filling in centre of wonton wrapper. Brush wrapper around filling with water. Fold wrapper over filling. Pinch and pleat wrapper together around filling to seal. Repeat with remaining filling and wrappers. Makes 20 wontons.

Wor Wonton Soup *A Classic!*

Chinese dried mushrooms	2	2
Boiling water	1 cup	250 mL
Cans of condensed chicken broth (10 oz., 284 mL, each)	3	3
Water	3 cups	750 mL
Coarsely grated carrot	2 tbsp.	30 mL
Boneless pork loin, cut julienne into 1 1/2 inch (3.8 cm) lengths (see Tip, page 60)	4 oz.	113 g
Raw medium shrimp, peeled and deveined	12	12
Fresh pea pods, cut in half	12	12
Shredded spinach, lightly packed	1/2 cup	125 mL
Green onions, sliced	2	2
Wontons	20	20
Boiling water	12 cups	3 L

Put mushrooms into small bowl. Add first amount of boiling water. Let stand for 20 minutes until softened. Strain through fine cloth or several layers of cheesecloth, reserving liquid. Remove and discard stems. Slice caps thinly.

Combine reserved liquid, mushrooms and next 4 ingredients in large pot or Dutch oven. Bring to a boil. Reduce heat. Cover. Boil gently for about 5 minutes until pork is tender.

Add shrimp, pea pods, spinach and green onion. Cover. Boil gently for about 4 minutes until shrimp are pink and pea pods are tender-crisp.

(continued on next page)

Add wontons to second amount of boiling water in large saucepan. Boil gently, uncovered, for about 3 minutes, stirring gently occasionally, until wrapper clings to filling and filling is fully cooked. Drain. Add wontons to hot broth. Serve immediately, ensuring each bowl gets 3 or 4 wontons and 2 shrimp. Makes about 9 cups (2.25 L). Serves 6.

1 serving: 375 Calories; 2.7 g Total Fat (0.6 g Mono, 0.2 g Poly, 0.5 g Sat); 48 mg Cholesterol; 67 g Carbohydrate; 2 g Fibre; 18 g Protein; 1546 mg Sodium

Pictured below.

tip

You can often find uncooked frozen wontons in the freezer section of your grocery store or in Asian markets. You may also try calling your favourite Chinese restaurant and ask to buy uncooked wontons.

This simple soup makes a stimulating start to your meal. A gentle heat and a mild sour tang add to the complex flavours of the broth.

variation

Before dividing into individual servings, add 1/2 cup (125 mL) diced firm tofu and heat through.

tip

To julienne, cut into very thin strips that resemble matchsticks.

tip

For best results, beat the eggs in a small liquid measure. This way you can pour the eggs into the soup in a thin, even stream.

Hot and Sour Soup

Prepared chicken broth	6 cups	1.5 L
Boneless pork loin, cut julienne into 1 1/2 inch (3.8 cm) lengths (see Tip, left)	7 oz.	200 g
Sliced fresh white mushrooms	1 cup	250 mL
Water	1/2 cup	125 mL
Cornstarch	2 tbsp.	30 mL
White vinegar	3 tbsp.	50 mL
Soy sauce	2 tbsp.	30 mL
Chili paste (sambal oelek)	2 tsp.	10 mL
Pepper	1/4 tsp.	1 mL
Large egg	1	1
Green onions, sliced	2	2

Bring broth to a boil in large saucepan. Add pork. Return to a boil. Reduce heat. Cover. Boil gently for about 5 minutes until pork is tender.

Add mushrooms. Cover. Simmer for 10 minutes.

Stir water into cornstarch in small bowl. Add next 4 ingredients. Stir into pork mixture until boiling and slightly thickened.

Beat egg with fork in small cup. Add egg to pork mixture in thin stream, constantly stirring in circular motion until fine egg threads form.

Sprinkle individual servings with green onion. Makes about 7 cups (1.75 L). Serves 6.

1 serving: 120 Calories; 4.5 g Total Fat (1.9 g Mono, 0.6 g Poly, 1.5 g Sat); 54 mg Cholesterol; 5 g Carbohydrate; trace Fibre; 13 g Protein; 1277 mg Sodium

Pictured at right.

A delicious reincarnation for leftover pork—just toss it into this hearty soup for a warm, filling meal.

variation

In place of navy beans you can use white kidney beans, mixed beans, black-eyed peas or another bean of your choice.

Quick Leftover Pork Soup

Cooking oil	2 tsp.	10 mL
Chopped onion	1 1/2 cups	375 mL
Dry white (or alcohol-free) wine (optional)	1/4 cup	60 mL
Water	4 cups	1 L
Can of navy beans (with liquid)	19 oz.	540 mL
Can of Italian-style diced tomatoes (with juice)	14 oz.	398 mL
Diced leftover roast pork	2 cups	500 mL
Diced potato	2 cups	500 mL
Grated carrot	1/2 cup	125 mL
Vegetable bouillon powder	2 tbsp.	30 mL
Pepper	1/2 tsp.	2 mL
Chopped fresh basil (or 1 1/2 tsp., 7 mL, dried)	2 tbsp.	30 mL

Heat cooking oil in large pot or Dutch oven on medium. Add onion. Cook for 5 to 10 minutes, stirring often, until softened.

Add wine. Bring to a boil. Boil for 1 minute.

Add next 8 ingredients. Stir. Bring to a boil. Reduce heat to medium-low. Cover. Simmer for about 45 minutes until potato is soft.

Stir in basil. Makes 9 cups (2.25 L).

1 cup (250 mL): 329 Calories; 5.0 g Total Fat (2.0 g Mono, 1.2 g Poly, 1.2 g Sat); 27 mg Cholesterol; 48 g Carbohydrate; 16 g Fibre; 24 g Protein; 888 mg Sodium

Pizza Topping Soup

Cooking oil	1 tsp.	5 mL
Hot Italian sausages, casings removed, chopped	1 lb.	454 g
Cans of diced tomatoes (with juice), 14 oz. (398 mL) each	2	2
Sliced fresh white mushrooms	2 cups	500 mL
Sliced green pepper	1 3/4 cups	425 mL
Can of condensed beef broth	10 oz.	284 mL
Chopped onion	1 cup	250 mL
Water	1 cup	250 mL
Can of tomato sauce	7 1/2 oz.	213 mL
Dried oregano	1/2 tsp.	2 mL
Dried basil	1/2 tsp.	2 mL
Cayenne pepper	1/8 tsp.	0.5 mL
Grated part-skim mozzarella cheese	1 cup	250 mL

Heat cooking oil in medium frying pan on medium. Add sausage. Scramble-fry for 8 to 10 minutes until no longer pink. Drain. Transfer to 4 to 5 quart (4 to 5 L) slow cooker.

Add next 10 ingredients. Stir well. Cover. Cook on Low for 8 to 9 hours or on High for 4 to 4 1/2 hours. Makes about 9 1/3 cups (2.3 L) soup.

Ladle soup into 6 individual bowls. Sprinkle each with cheese. Serves 6.

1 serving: 242 Calories; 13.3 g Total Fat (5.3 g Mono, 1.6 g Poly, 5.5 g Sat); 40 mg Cholesterol; 16 g Carbohydrate; 3 g Fibre; 16 g Protein; 1182 mg Sodium

Enjoy all the pizza toppings you love in a soup, all topped with melted mozzarella—just like a slice of your favourite pizza.

make ahead

The night before, prepare the tomato mixture. Chill overnight in a covered bowl. Assemble and cook as directed the next day.

serving suggestion

Serve with focaccia or crusty bread for dipping.

Hot sausage and vegetables in a rich, red broth with robust flavour—this soup can be served with bread or buns to make a complete meal. Ham replaces the more traditional salt cod in this recipe.

Portuguese Chowder

Hot sausage (such as chorizo or hot Italian)	1/2 lb.	225 g
Chopped onion	1 cup	250 mL
Garlic cloves, minced (or 1/2 tsp., 2 mL, powder)	2	2
Olive (or cooking) oil	1 tbsp.	15 mL
Can of diced tomatoes, with juice	28 oz.	796 mL
Water	3 cups	750 mL
Diced potato	2 cups	500 mL
Diced celery	1 cup	250 mL
Diced carrot	1 cup	250 mL
Beef bouillon powder	1 tbsp.	15 mL
Finely chopped cabbage	2 cups	500 mL
Diced cooked ham	1 cup	250 mL
Can of kidney beans, with liquid	14 oz.	398 mL
Dry red (or alcohol-free) wine (optional)	1/2 cup	125 mL

Remove sausage meat from casing. Scramble-fry sausage, onion and garlic in olive oil in large pot or Dutch oven until sausage is no longer pink and onion is soft.

Add next 6 ingredients. Bring to a boil. Reduce heat. Simmer, covered, for 20 minutes until vegetables are cooked.

Add cabbage, ham and kidney beans. Simmer, covered, for 15 minutes until cabbage is tender.

Stir in red wine. Makes 12 cups (3 L).

1 cup (250 mL): 155 Calories; 6.0 g Total Fat (1.2 g Mono, 0.2 g Poly, 1.8 g Sat); 17 mg Cholesterol; 16 g Carbohydrate; 3 g Fibre; 7 g Protein; 813 mg Sodium

Pictured at right.

The favourite flavour combination of ham and cheese in a soup! This kid-friendly chowder is simple to prepare and has a quick cooking time—perfect for lunch.

Ham and Cheese Chowder

Butter (or hard margarine)	2 tbsp.	30 mL
Chopped onion	1 cup	250 mL
All-purpose flour	2 tbsp.	30 mL
Dill weed	1/2 tsp.	2 mL
Pepper	1/4 tsp.	1 mL
Chicken Stock (page 26), or prepared chicken broth	2 cups	500 mL
Diced peeled potato	2 cups	500 mL
Grated medium Cheddar cheese	2 cups	500 mL
Milk	1 cup	250 mL
Diced cooked ham	1 cup	250 mL

Melt butter in large saucepan on medium. Add onion. Cook for 5 to 10 minutes, stirring often, until softened.

Add next 3 ingredients. Heat and stir for 1 minute.

Slowly stir in stock until combined. Heat and stir until boiling and thickened.

Add potato. Stir. Bring to a boil. Reduce heat to medium-low. Simmer, partially covered, for 15 to 20 minutes, stirring occasionally, until potato is tender.

Add remaining 3 ingredients. Heat and stir for about 5 minutes until heated through. Makes about 5 cups (1.25 L).

1 cup (250 mL): 390 Calories; 24.1 g Total Fat (7.3 g Mono, 1.1 g Poly, 14.5 g Sat); 82 mg Cholesterol; 21 g Carbohydrate; 2 g Fibre; 23 g Protein; 1165 mg Sodium

Polish Sauerkraut Soup

Bacon slices, diced	4	4
Sweet and sour cut pork ribs, trimmed of fat and cut into 1-bone portions	1 1/2 lbs.	680 g
Garlic clove, minced (or 1/4 tsp., 1 mL, powder)	1	1
Seasoned salt	1/2 tsp.	2 mL
Paprika	1/2 tsp.	2 mL
Pepper	1/4 tsp.	1 mL
Water	6 cups	1.5 L
Cans of stewed tomatoes (with juice), 14 oz. (398 mL) each, slightly mashed	2	2
Jar of sauerkraut, rinsed and drained well	17 1/2 oz.	500 mL
Large onion, chopped	1	1
Sliced carrot	1 cup	250 mL
Bay leaf	1	1
Can of small white beans, rinsed and drained	19 oz.	540 mL
Medium potato, diced	1	1

Cook bacon in large pot or Dutch oven on medium-high for about 5 minutes until starting to brown.

Add next 5 ingredients. Heat and stir for about 6 minutes until ribs are browned.

Add next 6 ingredients. Bring to a boil. Reduce heat to medium-low. Cover. Simmer for about 1 hour until ribs are tender. Remove and discard bay leaf.

Add beans and potato. Bring to a boil. Reduce heat to medium. Cover. Simmer for about 30 minutes until potato is tender but still holds its shape. Chill, covered, overnight if desired. Skim off and discard fat from surface before reheating. Makes about 14 cups (3.5 L).

1 cup (250 mL): 332 Calories; 6.1 g Total Fat (2.6 g Mono, 0.8 g Poly, 2.1 g Sat); 14 mg Cholesterol; 31 g Carbohydrate; 8 g Fibre; 19 g Protein; 495 mg Sodium

This mildly flavoured soup is thick with chunky vegetables, beans and ribs. Smoky bacon and tomato go well with the hearty ingredients.

food fun

Sauerkraut is regarded as a speciality of Germany, but did you know that soured cabbage and other soured vegetable dishes are also enjoyed in Eastern Europe, Russia, the Balkans, Hungary, Italy, Northern China, Chile, Turkey, Korea, Japan, the Phillipines and Indonesia? In the 18th century, sauerkraut even became a staple of British and German sailors' diets because its high vitamin C content and long shelf life helped prevent scurvy.

Put those harvest veggies to good use and warm up with this chunky tomato soup, thick with beans and bacon.

make ahead

The night before, combine first 10 ingredients in slow cooker liner. Cover, chill overnight and then cook as directed.

variation

Omit rosemary sprigs. Add 1/2 tsp. (2 mL) dried crushed rosemary to first 10 ingredients.

Hearty Winter Soup

Bacon slices, cooked crisp and crumbled	8	8
Prepared chicken broth	6 cups	1.5 L
Chopped yellow turnip	3 cups	750 mL
Can of white kidney beans, rinsed and drained	19 oz.	540 mL
Chopped onion	1 cup	250 mL
Chopped carrot	1 cup	250 mL
Chopped celery	1/2 cup	125 mL
Tomato paste (see Tip, page 22)	1/4 cup	60 mL
Salt	1/4 tsp.	1 mL
Pepper	1/4 tsp.	1 mL
Frozen peas	1 cup	250 mL
Sprigs of fresh rosemary	2	2
Chopped fresh parsley (or 1 1/2 tsp., 7 mL, flakes)	2 tbsp.	30 mL
Lemon juice	1 tbsp.	15 mL

Combine first 10 ingredients in 5 to 7 quart (5 to 7 L) slow cooker. Cover. Cook on Low for 9 to 10 hours or on High for 4 1/2 to 5 hours.

Add remaining 4 ingredients. Stir well. Cover. Cook on High for about 10 minutes until peas are heated through. Remove and discard rosemary sprigs. Makes about 11 cups (2.75 L).

1 cup (250 mL): 119 Calories; 3.4 g Total Fat (1.5 g Mono, 0.6 g Poly, 1.1 g Sat); 4 mg Cholesterol; 15 g Carbohydrate; 4 g Fibre; 8 g Protein; 690 mg Sodium

Pictured at right.

Not too thin, not too heavy, and loaded with flavour. Cream and potatoes mellow the spicy bite of Mexican sausage and chilies.

about kale

Kale might once have been considered a lowly vegetable, but not anymore. It's packed with nutrition and antioxidants, it's beautiful enough to plant just for its good looks, it grows superbly even in quite cold climates and it can be harvested early or later in the season—in fact it tastes sweeter after a light frost. You can use it as a substitute for other greens such as spinach and chard as well. It's hard not to love a vegetable with this many virtues.

storing kale tip

If you're not sure what to do with leftover kale, try cutting out the ribs and freezing the leaves. Once they're frozen, they can be broken up very easily and measured out for use in soups and sauces.

Creamy Kale Soup

Ingredient	Imperial	Metric
Bacon slices, diced	2	2
Chorizo sausage, casing removed, chopped	8 oz.	225 g
Diced onion	1 cup	250 mL
Garlic cloves, minced (or 1/2 tsp., 2 mL, powder)	2	2
All-purpose flour	2 tsp.	10 mL
Chicken Stock (page 26), or prepared chicken broth	6 cups	1.5 L
Dried crushed chilies	1/4 tsp.	1 mL
Medium unpeeled baking potatoes	2	2
Shredded kale leaves, lightly packed	1 cup	250 mL
Half-and-half cream	1 cup	250 mL
Grated Parmesan cheese, for garnish		

Cook bacon in large saucepan on medium until almost crisp. Add sausage. Scramble-fry for about 5 minutes until sausage is browned. Transfer sausage and bacon with slotted spoon to paper towel-lined plate to drain. Set aside.

Heat 2 tsp. (10 mL) drippings in same saucepan on medium. Add onion and garlic. Cook for 5 to 10 minutes, stirring often, until onion is softened.

Sprinkle with flour. Heat and stir for 1 minute. Add stock and chilies. Stir. Bring to a boil.

Cut potatoes in half lengthwise. Cut crosswise into 1/4 inch (6 mm) slices, making half moons. Add to stock. Boil gently, partially covered, for 10 minutes until potato is almost tender.

Add kale and sausage mixture. Boil gently, partially covered, for 5 minutes. Remove from heat.

Add cream. Stir. Garnish individual servings with Parmesan cheese. Makes about 9 cups (2.25 L).

1 cup (250 mL): 289 Calories; 14.6 g Total Fat (6.2 g Mono, 1.2 g Poly, 6.4 g Sat); 3 mg Cholesterol; 15 g Carbohydrate; 1 g Fibre; 10 g Protein; 924 mg Sodium

Pictured at right.

A warm, hearty soup filled with lots of beans, deep green spinach and colourful vegetables.

variation

In place of navy beans you can use white kidney beans, mixed beans, black-eyed peas or another bean of your choice.

Hearty Ham Bone Soup | *A Classic!*

Water	10 cups	2.5 L
Leftover meaty ham bone	1	1
Celery ribs, diced	4	4
Medium carrots, sliced	3	3
Medium onions, chopped	2	2
Bay leaf	1	1
Parsley flakes	1 tbsp.	15 mL
Salt	2 tsp.	10 mL
Coarse ground pepper	1/4 tsp.	1 mL
Medium potatoes, peeled and diced	2	2
Can of mixed beans, rinsed and drained	19 oz.	540 mL
Can of navy beans, rinsed, drained and slightly mashed with fork	14 oz.	398 mL
Chopped fresh spinach, stems removed, lightly packed (optional)	1 cup	250 mL

Put water and ham bone into large pot or Dutch oven. Bring to a boil. Boil, uncovered, for 5 minutes. Carefully skim off and discard foam from surface. Return to a boil.

Add next 7 ingredients. Reduce heat to medium-low. Cover. Simmer for about 2 hours until ham is falling off bone. Remove all meat from bone. Discard bone. Chop meat. Return to soup. Remove and discard bay leaf.

Add potato, mixed beans and navy beans. Bring to a boil. Reduce heat to medium-low. Cover. Simmer for about 20 minutes until potatoes are tender.

Add spinach. Cook for 5 minutes. Makes 12 cups (3 L). Serves 8.

1 serving: 335 Calories; 3.5 g Total Fat (1.2 g Mono, 0.8 g Poly, 0.9 g Sat); 23 mg Cholesterol; 52 g Carbohydrate; 17 g Fibre; 27 g Protein; 1259 mg Sodium

Pictured at right.

This delicious lamb and bean soup has a savoury, complex broth. Made in the slow cooker, it is a meal in itself.

about bouquet garni

A traditional bouquet garni is a bunch of herbs tied together to make them easy to remove before you serve the dish, so you get all the flavour without the fuss. We've used a combination of dried herbs and spices, so we've wrapped them in cheesecloth to keep them in a tidy bundle.

variation

In place of navy beans you can use white kidney beans, mixed beans, black-eyed peas or another bean of your choice.

Lamb Bouquet Soup

Dried navy beans	1 cup	250 mL
Beef Stock (page 6), or prepared beef broth	7 cups	1.75 L
Lamb shanks (about 1 1/2 lbs., 680 g)	2	2
Chopped onion	1 cup	250 mL
Chopped celery	1 cup	250 mL
Pot barley	1/2 cup	125 mL
Sliced carrot	1/2 cup	125 mL
Chopped fresh rosemary (or 1/2 tsp., 2 mL, dried, crushed)	2 tsp.	10 mL
Paprika	1/2 tsp.	2 mL
ALLSPICE BOUQUET GARNI		
Bay leaves	2	2
Whole allspice	2	2
Fresh parsley sprigs	2	2
Whole black peppercorns	8	8
Garlic clove	1	1
Diced fresh tomato	1 1/2 cups	375 mL
Brown sugar, packed	2 tbsp.	30 mL
Grated lemon zest	1 tsp.	5 mL
Salt	1/2 tsp.	2 mL

Measure beans into small heatproof bowl. Add boiling water until 2 inches (5 cm) above beans. Let stand for at least 1 hour until cool. Drain. Rinse beans. Drain. Transfer to 5 to 7 quart (5 to 7 L) slow cooker.

Add next 8 ingredients. Stir.

Allspice Bouquet Garni: Place first 5 ingredients on 10 inch (25 cm) square piece of cheesecloth. Draw up corners and tie with butcher's string. Submerge in liquid in slow cooker. Cook, covered, on Low for about 10 hours or on High for about 5 hours until beans are tender and lamb is falling off bones. Remove and discard bouquet garni. Remove shanks to cutting board using slotted spoon. Keep bean mixture covered. Remove lamb from bones. Discard bones. Chop lamb coarsely. Return to slow cooker.

Add remaining 4 ingredients. Stir. Cook, covered, on High for about 15 minutes until heated through. Makes about 12 cups (3 L).

1 cup (250 mL): 247 Calories; 10.4 g Total Fat (4.1 g Mono, 1.0 g Poly, 4.4 g Sat); 33 mg Cholesterol; 23 g Carbohydrate; 5 g Fibre; 15 g Protein; 639 mg Sodium

Scotch Broth *A Classic!*

Water	8 cups	2 L
Lamb stew meat, cut into small pieces	1 lb.	454 g
Pearl or pot barley	1/2 cup	125 mL
Diced yellow turnip	1 cup	250 mL
Diced carrot	2 cups	500 mL
Medium onions, chopped	2	2
Leeks, white part only, sliced (optional)	2	2
Shredded cabbage, packed	2 cups	500 mL
Chopped celery	1/2 cup	125 mL
Salt	2 tsp.	10 mL
Pepper	1/2 tsp.	2 mL
Thyme	1/4 tsp.	1 mL

Put water, lamb and barley into large saucepan. Bring to a boil. Cover and simmer 1 hour.

Add remaining 9 ingredients. Stir. Bring to a boil again. Cover and simmer about 30 minutes. Makes about 12 cups (3 L).

1 cup (250 mL): 105 Calories; 2.3 g Total Fat (0.8 g Mono, 0.2 g Poly, 0.7 g Sat); 25 mg Cholesterol; 12 g Carbohydrate; 3 g Fibre; 9 g Protein; 442 mg Sodium

Pictured below.

This Scottish soup is made with lots of vegetables and thickened with barley. It is traditionally made with lamb, but beef may also be used. This thick soup may be thinned with water if you prefer, but be sure to adjust the seasonings.

about barley

A grain cultivated since ancient times, barley is low in gluten and has many culinary uses. Pearl barley has had the husk, bran and germ removed, making it faster-cooking with a smoother texture, but also making it less nutritious than whole barley. Pot or Scotch barley has had only the husk removed, so it's coarser and chewier than pearl barley, but it also retains some bran, B vitamins and potassium. Either one works well in Scotch Broth.

This classic beet soup has the gorgeous colour you've come to expect, and is especially thrifty if you make it with vegetables from your own garden. Garnish with a sprinkle of fresh dill.

serving suggestion

Highlight the beautiful colour of beet soup by serving it in plain white bowls or in a simple soup tureen in a contrasting colour.

tip

Don't get caught red-handed! Wear rubber gloves when handling beets.

Borscht *A Classic!*

Grated beets (about 1 1/2 lbs., 680 g), see Tip, left	5 cups	1.25 L
Chopped onion	1 1/2 cups	375 mL
Hot water	10 cups	2.5 L
Vegetable bouillon powder	2 tbsp.	30 mL
Coarsely grated cabbage	2 cups	500 mL
Celery rib, diced	1	1
Medium carrot, grated	1	1
Medium potato, grated	1	1
Granulated sugar	1 tsp.	5 mL
Salt	1 tsp.	5 mL
Pepper	1/4 tsp.	1 mL
Bay leaf	1	1
Dill weed	1 1/2 tsp.	7 mL
Garlic powder	1/4 tsp.	1 mL
Apple cider vinegar	1/4 cup	60 mL
Sour cream, for garnish	3/4 cup	175 mL

Combine first 15 ingredients in large heavy pot or Dutch oven. Bring to a boil, stirring often. Reduce heat. Cover. Boil gently for about 1 hour, stirring occasionally, until slightly reduced. Remove and discard bay leaf.

Top individual servings with dollop of sour cream. Makes about 15 cups (3.75 L).

1 cup (250 mL): 41 Calories; 0.1 g Total Fat (trace Mono, 0.1 g Poly, trace Sat); 0 mg Cholesterol; 10 g Carbohydrate; 2 g Fibre; 1 g Protein; 653 mg Sodium

Pictured below.

Garden Fresh Tomato Soup

Medium tomatoes (about 3 lbs., 1.4 kg)	8	8
Cooking oil	2 tsp.	10 mL
Chopped onion	1 cup	250 mL
Chopped carrot	1/2 cup	125 mL
Chopped celery	1/2 cup	125 mL
Garlic cloves, minced (or 1/2 tsp., 2 mL, powder)	2	2
Chicken Stock (page 26), or prepared chicken broth	1 cup	250 mL
Tomato paste (see Tip, page 22)	2 tbsp.	30 mL
Granulated sugar	2 tsp.	10 mL
Dried basil	1/2 tsp.	2 mL
Dried oregano	1/2 tsp.	2 mL
Dried thyme	1/2 tsp.	2 mL
Bay leaf	1	1
Salt	1/2 tsp.	2 mL
Pepper	1/2 tsp.	2 mL

Cut 'X' through skin on bottom of tomatoes. Place tomatoes in boiling water in large saucepan for 30 seconds. Transfer to ice water in large bowl using slotted spoon. Let stand until cool enough to handle. Peel and discard skins. Cut each tomato into quarters. Remove seeds. Chop tomato. Set aside. Discard cooking water.

Heat cooking oil in same saucepan on medium. Add next 4 ingredients. Cook for 5 to 10 minutes, stirring occasionally, until vegetables are softened.

Add tomato and remaining 9 ingredients. Stir. Bring to a boil. Reduce heat to medium-low. Simmer, covered, for about 30 minutes, stirring occasionally, until vegetables are very soft. Discard bay leaf. Carefully process with hand blender or in blender until smooth (see Safety Tip). Makes about 5 cups (1.25 L).

1 cup (250 mL): 114 Calories; 3.0 g Total Fat (1.3 g Mono, 1.0 g Poly, 0.4 g Sat); 0 mg Cholesterol; 22 g Carbohydrate; 5 g Fibre; 4 g Protein; 461 mg Sodium

Safety Tip: Follow manufacturer's instructions for processing hot liquids.

Forget the canned tomatoes—this soup is a tangy treat full of fresh veggies. Perfect for when your kitchen is overflowing with harvested garden tomatoes.

cream of tomato soup

Add 1/2 cup (125 mL) whipping cream after processing. Heat and stir until heated through.

A nice and thick tomato soup that warms the body and the soul! Creamy tomato and vegetable flavours blend to create a delectable version of this favourite.

Mom's Creamed Tomato Soup   *A Classic!*

Chopped onion	1/2 cup	125 mL
Chopped celery	1/2 cup	125 mL
Hard margarine (or butter)	1 tbsp.	15 mL
Water	1 cup	250 mL
Cans of stewed tomatoes (14 oz., 398 mL, each)	2	2
Chicken (or vegetable) bouillon powder	1 tbsp.	15 mL
Granulated sugar	1/2 tsp.	2 mL
Pepper	1/8 tsp.	0.5 mL
Homogenized milk	1 cup	250 mL
All-purpose flour	2 tbsp.	30 mL

Cheddar cheese fish crackers (optional)

Sauté onion and celery in margarine in medium saucepan for about 4 minutes until onion is soft and clear.

Add water, tomatoes, bouillon powder, sugar and pepper. Bring to a boil. Reduce heat. Simmer, partially covered, for 30 minutes. Purée in blender or with hand blender until smooth (see Safety Tip). Return to saucepan.

Gradually whisk milk into flour in small bowl until smooth. Add to tomato mixture. Heat and stir on medium until boiling and slightly thickened. Ladle into individual soup bowls.

Top with crackers. Makes 5 cups (1.25 L).

1 cup (250 mL): 112 Calories; 4.1 g Total Fat (1.2 g Mono, 0.2 g Poly, 2.5 g Sat); 14 mg Cholesterol; 16 g Carbohydrate; trace Fibre; 4 g Protein; 1070 mg Sodium

Safety Tip: Follow manufacturer's instructions for processing hot liquids.

Tomato Gin Soup

Cooking oil	1 tsp.	5 mL
Chopped onion	1 cup	250 mL
Chopped celery	1/2 cup	125 mL
Garlic clove, minced	1	1
(or 1/4 tsp., 1 mL, powder)		
Jalapeño pepper, finely diced	1	1
(see Tip, page 15)		
Tomato juice	4 cups	1 L
Can of diced tomatoes (with juice)	14 oz.	398 mL
Water	1 1/2 cups	375 mL
Worcestershire sauce	1 tbsp.	15 mL
Grated lime zest (see Tip, page 104)	1 tsp.	5 mL
Gin	1/3 cup	75 mL
Lime juice	1/4 cup	60 mL
Liquid honey	1 tbsp.	15 mL

Heat cooking oil in large saucepan on medium. Add next 4 ingredients. Cook for 5 to 10 minutes, stirring often, until onion and celery are softened.

Add next 5 ingredients. Bring to a boil. Reduce heat to medium-low. Simmer, partially covered, for about 15 minutes, stirring occasionally, until vegetables are tender. Carefully process with hand blender or in blender until smooth (see Safety Tip).

Add remaining 3 ingredients. Stir. Makes about 8 cups (2 L).

1 cup (250 mL): 83 Calories; 0.8 g Total Fat (0.4 g Mono, 0.3 g Poly, 0.1 g Sat); 0 mg Cholesterol; 14 g Carbohydrate; 2 g Fibre; 2 g Protein; 579 mg Sodium

Safety Tip: Follow manufacturer's instructions for processing hot liquids.

A tipple of gin adds a cheeky flair to this fun, fresh and inviting lime and tomato soup.

about gin

Gin is an alcoholic spirit distilled from grains. It is closely associated with juniper, as it is infused with the essence of the bitter berries of this plant. In France, gin is known as *genièvre,* which is also French for "juniper berry."

That's "garlic soup" to you! The mellow, roasted garlic flavour is subtly sweet in this rich yet light soup.

Zuppa d'Aglio

Large garlic bulb	1	1
Olive (or cooking) oil	2 tbsp.	30 mL
Small onion, chopped	1	1
Large celery rib, chopped	1	1
Dry white (or alcohol-free) wine	1/2 cup	125 mL
Chicken Stock (page 26), or prepared chicken broth	8 cups	2 L
All-purpose flour	2 tbsp.	30 mL
Water	2 cups	500 mL
Small potato, peeled and cut into 6 pieces	1	1
Whipping cream (or homogenized milk)	1/2 cup	125 mL
Chopped fresh basil (or 3/4 tsp., 4 mL, dried)	1 tbsp.	15 mL
Chopped fresh thyme leaves (or 1/4 tsp., 1 mL, dried)	1 tsp.	5 mL
Salt	1 tsp.	5 mL
Hot pepper sauce	1/2 tsp.	2 mL

Chopped fresh parsley, for garnish
Coarsely ground pepper, for garnish

Cut garlic bulb in half horizontally. Remove any loose, papery outer skins. Preheat gas barbecue or frying pan to medium. Cook bulb halves, cut sides down, on greased grill or in small greased frying pan until exposed garlic is very brown. Cool until able to handle. Peel and separate garlic cloves.

Heat olive oil in large pot or Dutch oven on medium-high. Cook onion, celery and garlic cloves, stirring constantly, until all are golden.

Add wine. Boil, uncovered, for 2 minutes.

Stir 1/3 cup (75 mL) stock into flour in small cup until smooth. Add to onion mixture. Add remaining stock and water. Stir. Add potato. Bring to a boil, stirring constantly. Reduce heat to medium. Cover. Boil gently for 1 hour. Strain solids from liquid, returning liquid to pot. Purée solids in blender or food processor (see Safety Tip). Add purée to liquid. Bring to a boil.

(continued on next page)

Add whipping cream, basil, thyme, salt and hot pepper sauce. Stir until heated through. Do not boil. Remove from heat.

Sprinkle individual servings with parsley and pepper. Makes 8 cups (2 L). Serves 6.

1 serving: 224 Calories; 13.9 g Total Fat (6.5 g Mono, 1.1 g Poly, 5.8 g Sat); 27 mg Cholesterol; 13 g Carbohydrate; 1 g Fibre; 8 g Protein; 1449 mg Sodium

Pictured below.

Safety Tip: Follow manufacturer's instructions for processing hot liquids.

Muhl-ih-guh-TAW-nee, which means "pepper water," is a traditional soup from India—a creamy, warmly spiced medley of potatoes, apples, lentils and onions. Garnish with yogurt and sprigs of fresh cilantro.

time-saving tip

If you've no time to make stock from scratch, make a quick substitute by using 8 cups (2 L) water plus 3 tbsp. (50 mL) chicken bouillon powder.

tip

To bruise cardamom, pound pods with mallet or press with flat side of wide knife to "bruise," or crack them open slightly.

Mulligatawny Soup

Chopped onion	1 1/2 cups	375 mL
Garlic cloves, minced (or 1/2 tsp., 2 mL, powder)	2	2
Finely grated ginger root (or 1/2 tsp., 2 mL, ground ginger)	2 tsp.	10 mL
Fresh small chilies, chopped (see Tip, page 15)	2	2
Curry powder	1 tbsp.	15 mL
Ground cumin	1/4 – 2 tsp.	1 – 10 mL
Ground coriander	1/4 – 2 tsp.	1 – 10 mL
Canola oil	2 tsp.	10 mL
Cinnamon stick (4 inch, 10 cm, length)	1	1
Whole green cardamom, bruised (see Tip, left)	6 – 8	6 – 8
Red lentils	1 1/4 cups	300 mL
Chicken Stock (page 26), or prepared chicken broth	8 cups	2 L
Medium potatoes, peeled and chopped	2	2
Medium cooking apples (such as McIntosh), peeled, cored and chopped	2	2
Buttermilk	1 1/2 cups	375 mL
Fresh cilantro leaves	3 tbsp.	50 mL

Sauté first 7 ingredients in canola oil in large pot or Dutch oven for about 5 minutes until onion is soft.

Add next 6 ingredients. Stir. Bring to a boil. Reduce heat to medium-low. Cover. Simmer for about 25 minutes, stirring occasionally, until lentils and potato are soft. Cool slightly. Remove and discard cinnamon stick and cardamom. Process in blender, in 2 to 3 batches, until smooth (see Safety Tip). Return to pot.

Add buttermilk and cilantro. Heat and stir on medium for 5 to 7 minutes until heated through. Makes about 12 cups (3 L).

1 cup (250 mL): 162 Calories; 2.9 g Total Fat (1.1 g Mono, 0.5 g Poly, 0.7 g Sat); 2 mg Cholesterol; 24 g Carbohydrate; 5 g Fibre; 11 g Protein; 548 mg Sodium

Pictured at right.

Safety Tip: Follow manufacturer's instructions for processing hot liquids.

A classic, warming soup with delicious caramelized onions and a savoury herb undertone. Be sure to remind everyone—the bowls will be very hot!

about french onion soup bowls

While French onion soup can be served in any broiler-proof serving bowls, this soup has become associated with distinctive oven-to-table dishes. The most familiar design has a single handle to help transport the hot bowls, but another variation, called a lion's head, has small handles on each side. French onion soup bowls were traditionally made of brown ceramic, but they now come in a variety of colours and can be made from porcelain, stoneware and earthenware.

French Onion Soup

Onions, peeled (about 8 medium)	2 lbs.	900 g
Hard margarine (or butter)	2 tbsp.	30 mL
Salt	1 tsp.	5 mL
Garlic cloves, minced (or 1 tsp., 5 mL, powder)	4	4
Coarsely ground pepper (or 1/4 tsp., 1 mL, pepper)	1/2 tsp.	2 mL
Dry sherry	1/2 cup	125 mL
Bay leaves	3	3
Fresh thyme sprigs	3	3
Prepared beef broth	4 cups	1 L
Multi-grain rye bread slices, cut about 1/3 inch (1 cm) thick and lightly toasted or air-dried	8	8
Grated Gruyère cheese	1 1/3 cups	325 mL

Cut each onion in half lengthwise. Lay flat side on cutting board. Cut crosswise into 1/8 inch (3 mm) slices.

Melt margarine in large pot or Dutch oven on medium-low. Add onion and salt. Stir. Cover. Cook for about 45 minutes, stirring occasionally, until onion is soft, but not browned.

Add garlic and pepper. Stir. Cook, uncovered, on medium-high, stirring frequently and scraping bottom of pot, until onion is deep caramel brown.

Add sherry. Stir well, scraping any browning from pot and blending with liquid.

Add bay leaves, thyme sprigs and broth. Bring to a boil. Reduce heat to medium-low. Cover. Simmer for 30 minutes, without stirring. Remove and discard bay leaves and thyme sprigs. Makes about 5 cups (1.25 L) soup.

Arrange 4 ovenproof serving bowls on baking sheet with sides. Place 2 slices of bread in each. Ladle soup over bread, allowing 1 to 2 minutes for bread to soak up liquid.

Sprinkle each with cheese. Broil until cheese is browned and bubbly. Let stand for 5 minutes. Carefully transfer hot soup bowls to plates. Serves 4.

1 serving: 532 Calories; 19.7 g Total Fat (5.2 g Mono, 1.0 g Poly, 10.6 g Sat); 55 mg Cholesterol; 67 g Carbohydrate; 7 g Fibre; 22 g Protein; 2448 mg Sodium

Pictured at right.

A light starter soup with earthy mushrooms and fresh chives—perfect for priming the appetite for a main course.

Mushroom Consommé

Package of dried porcini mushrooms	3/4 oz.	22 g
Boiling water	1 cup	250 mL
Prepared beef broth	4 cups	1 L
Bay leaf	1	1
Whole clove	1	1
Butter (or hard margarine)	2 tsp.	10 mL
Sliced fresh brown (or white) mushrooms	2 cups	500 mL
Chopped fresh chives	2 tbsp.	30 mL
(or 1 1/2 tsp., 7 mL, dried)		
Dry sherry	1 tbsp.	15 mL
Lemon juice	1 tsp.	5 mL

Put dried mushrooms into small heatproof bowl. Add boiling water. Stir. Let stand for about 15 minutes until softened. Remove mushrooms. Strain liquid through triple layer of cheesecloth into large saucepan. Finely chop mushrooms and stems. Set aside.

Add next 3 ingredients to saucepan. Bring to a boil. Reduce heat to medium-low. Simmer, covered, for 15 minutes to blend flavours.

Melt butter in large frying pan on medium. Add brown and porcini mushrooms. Cook for about 10 minutes, stirring often, until mushrooms are browned and liquid is evaporated. Add to broth mixture.

Add remaining 3 ingredients. Stir. Discard bay leaf and clove. Makes about 5 cups (1.25 L). Serves 6.

1 serving: 36 Calories; 1.6 g Total Fat (0.4 g Mono, 0.1 g Poly, 0.9 g Sat); 3 mg Cholesterol; 3 g Carbohydrate; 1 g Fibre; 2 g Protein; 784 mg Sodium

Creamy Mushroom Soup *A Classic!*

Sliced fresh mushrooms (your favourite)	6 cups	1.5 L
Cooking oil	2 tsp.	10 mL
Pepper, sprinkle		
Cooking oil	2 tsp.	10 mL
Chopped green onion	1/2 cup	125 mL
Garlic cloves, minced	2	2
All-purpose flour	3 tbsp.	50 mL
Low-sodium prepared chicken broth	2 cups	500 mL
Milk	2 cups	500 mL
Dry (or alcohol-free) white wine	1/4 cup	60 mL
Reduced-sodium chicken bouillon powder	2 tsp.	10 mL
Pepper	1/4 tsp.	1 mL
Ground thyme (optional)	1/8 tsp.	0.5 mL

A long-time favourite you'll make again and again. Make it chunky or smooth to suit your preference—it's delicious either way.

Put mushrooms into medium bowl. Add first amount of cooking oil. Stir until coated. Spread in single layer in greased baking sheet with sides. Sprinkle with first amount of pepper. Bake in 400°F (205°C) oven for about 10 minutes until mushrooms are softened. Do not drain.

Heat second amount of cooking oil in large pot or Dutch oven on medium. Add green onion and garlic. Cook for about 5 minutes, stirring often, until green onion is softened.

Add flour. Heat and stir for 1 minute. Slowly add next 3 ingredients, stirring constantly until boiling and thickened.

Add mushrooms with liquid and remaining 3 ingredients. Heat and stir for 3 to 4 minutes. Reduce heat to medium-low. Cover. Simmer for 5 minutes. Remove from heat. Cool slightly. Carefully process in blender or food processor until mushrooms are finely chopped (see Safety Tip). Return to same large pot. Heat and stir on medium for about 5 minutes until heated through. Makes 6 cups (1.5 L). Serves 6.

1 serving: 116 Calories; 4.5 g Total Fat (2.2 g Mono, 1.1 g Poly, 0.9 g Sat); 4 mg Cholesterol; 12 g Carbohydrate; 1 g Fibre; 6 g Protein; 392 mg Sodium

Safety Tip: Follow manufacturer's instructions for processing hot liquids.

An excellent soup that can be blended to whatever texture you like. Raid the garden and try it with homegrown carrots!

carrot chowder

Cook 1 1/3 cups (325 mL) diced potato along with the carrot and onion. Has a similar flavour but is a touch mellower.

curried carrot soup

Add 1/2 tsp. (2 mL) curry powder with flour. Has quite a mild flavour.

Cream of Carrot Soup

Peeled and cut up carrot	4 cups	1 L
Chicken Stock (page 26), or prepared broth	2 cups	500 mL
Chopped onion	1 cup	250 mL
Butter (or hard margarine)	3 tbsp.	50 mL
All-purpose flour	3 tbsp.	50 mL
Salt	1 tsp.	5 mL
Pepper	1/8 tsp.	0.5 mL
Seasoned salt	1/4 tsp.	1 mL
Milk	4 cups	1 L

Combine carrot, stock and onion in saucepan. Cook until vegetables are tender. Do not drain. Cool a bit. Run through blender (see Safety Tip). Set aside.

Melt butter in saucepan over medium heat. Stir in flour, salt, pepper and seasoned salt. Add milk. Heat and stir until it boils and thickens. Add carrot mixture. Reheat and serve. Makes 7 cups (1.75 L).

1 cup (250 mL): 167 Calories; 6.9 g Total Fat (2.0 g Mono, 0.4 g Poly, 4.1 g Sat); 21 mg Cholesterol; 19 g Carbohydrate; 2 g Fibre; 8 g Protein; 764 mg Sodium

Pictured on front cover.

Safety Tip: Follow manufacturer's instructions for processing hot liquids.

This thick and creamy soup has a distinctive pale green colour and the delicious fresh taste of asparagus.

Cream of Asparagus Soup

Fresh asparagus, trimmed of tough ends	1 1/2 lbs.	680 g
Water		
Chopped onion	3/4 cup	175 mL
Cooking oil	1 tbsp.	15 mL
Chicken bouillon powder	2 tsp.	10 mL
All-purpose flour	2 tbsp.	30 mL
Salt	3/4 tsp.	4 mL
Pepper (white is best)	1/4 tsp.	1 mL
Milk	2 cups	500 mL
Ground nutmeg, sprinkle (optional)		

(continued on next page)

Cook asparagus in water in large saucepan until tender. Drain. Reserve 4 spears for garnish. Cut remaining spears into 2 inch (5 cm) pieces. Return to saucepan.

Sauté onion in cooking oil in small frying pan until soft. Add to asparagus.

Combine bouillon powder, flour, salt and pepper in medium bowl. Stir in milk until smooth. Gradually stir into asparagus mixture. Heat and stir until boiling and thickened. Cool slightly. Put into blender. Process, in batches, until smooth (see Safety Tip). Return to saucepan. Heat through.

Garnish individual servings with reserved asparagus spears. Sprinkle with nutmeg. Makes 4 cups (1 L).

1 cup (250 mL): 150 Calories; 5.1 g Total Fat (2.6 g Mono, 1.2 g Poly, 1.1 g Sat); 8 mg Cholesterol; 20 g Carbohydrate; 4 g Fibre; 9 g Protein; 1062 mg Sodium

Pictured below.

Safety Tip: Follow manufacturer's instructions for processing hot liquids.

Cream of Asparagus Soup, left

about growing asparagus

Crazy about asparagus? Why not grow your own and enjoy tender spears every spring? Asparagus is a perennial plant in the lily family that can be grown relatively easily, with a bit of patience. Started from seed or planted as roots, called "crowns," asparagus will begin producing spears by the second or third spring. A properly cared for asparagus patch will be fruitful for many years.

Not to worry, we don't expect you to dine on your garden flora—it's simple green peas that impart a nice, sweet flavour to this soup. The tangy Minted Yogurt topping bumps it up to sensational.

minted yogurt

Plain yogurt	1/3 cup	75 mL
Chopped fresh mint	2 tbsp.	30 mL

Combine yogurt and mint in small bowl. Spoon onto individual servings of soup. Makes about 6 tbsp. (100 mL) yogurt.

Sweet Pea Soup

Olive (or canola) oil	2 tsp.	10 mL
Finely chopped green onion	1/2 cup	125 mL
Garlic clove, minced (or 1/4 tsp., 1 mL, powder)	1	1
Frozen peas	2 cups	500 mL
Chopped or torn green leaf lettuce, lightly packed	1 1/2 cups	375 mL
Low-sodium prepared chicken (or vegetable) broth	3 cups	750 mL
Pepper	1/4 tsp.	1 mL
Frozen peas	1/2 cup	125 mL

Heat olive oil in medium saucepan on medium. Add green onion and garlic. Cook for about 5 minutes, stirring occasionally, until green onion is softened.

Add first amount of peas and lettuce. Heat and stir for 1 minute.

Add broth and pepper. Bring to a boil. Reduce heat to medium-low. Simmer for 3 to 5 minutes, stirring occasionally, until peas are tender. Carefully process with hand blender or in blender until smooth (see Safety Tip).

Add second amount of peas. Heat and stir on medium for about 2 minutes until peas are tender. Makes about 4 1/2 cups (1.1 L) soup. Serves 4

1 serving with 1 1/2 tbsp. (25 mL) Minted Yogurt: 126 Calories; 3.8 g Total Fat (2.1 g Mono, 0.5 g Poly, 0.9 g Sat); 3 mg Cholesterol; 16 g Carbohydrate; 5 g Fibre; 8 g Protein; 144 mg Sodium

Safety Tip: Follow manufacturer's instructions for processing hot liquids.

Dill Pickle Soup

Butter (or hard margarine)	2 tbsp.	30 mL
Chopped peeled potato	2 cups	500 mL
Chopped onion	1 cup	250 mL
Chopped carrot	1 cup	250 mL
Pepper	1/4 tsp.	1 mL
All-purpose flour	2 tbsp.	30 mL
Chicken Stock (page 26), or prepared chicken broth	4 cups	1 L
Dill pickle juice	1/4 cup	60 mL
Half-and-half cream	1 cup	250 mL
Chopped dill pickles	2/3 cup	150 mL
Chopped fresh dill (or 1 tbsp., 15 mL, dill weed)	1/4 cup	60 mL
Sour cream	1/2 cup	125 mL

Melt butter in large saucepan on medium. Add next 4 ingredients. Stir. Cook, partially covered, for 8 to 10 minutes, stirring occasionally, until vegetables start to soften.

Sprinkle with flour. Heat and stir for 1 minute.

Slowly add 1 cup (250 mL) stock. Heat and stir until boiling and thickened. Add pickle juice and remaining stock. Cook, stirring often, until boiling. Reduce heat to medium-low. Simmer, covered, for about 15 minutes, stirring occasionally, until potato is tender.

Add cream and pickles. Stir. Cook for about 2 minutes until hot but not boiling.

Add dill. Carefully process with hand blender or in blender until smooth (see Safety Tip).

Spoon sour cream onto individual servings. Makes about 8 cups (2 L).

1 cup (250 mL): 152 Calories; 8.6 g Total Fat (2.4 g Mono, 0.4 g Poly, 5.4 g Sat); 24 mg Cholesterol; 16 g Carbohydrate; 2 g Fibre; 4 g Protein; 623 mg Sodium

Safety Tip: Follow manufacturer's instructions for processing hot liquids.

You're never in a pickle when you serve this fun and festive soup. Try adding cooked diced chicken, ham or sausage for extra protein.

serving suggestion

Dill Pickle Soup goes well with cheese sandwiches. Vary the cheese for different flavour combinations.

This wonderful soup has been a family favourite forever. Get it on the stove when you walk in the door and it'll be ready in a jiffy!

Corn Soup

Milk	3 1/2 cups	875 mL
Finely chopped onion	2 tbsp.	30 mL
Butter (or hard margarine)	1 tsp.	5 mL
Cans of cream-style corn (10 oz., 284 mL, each)	2	2
Milk	1/2 cup	125 mL
All-purpose flour	2 tbsp.	30 mL
Salt	1 tsp.	5 mL
Pepper	1/8 tsp.	0.5 mL

Butter, chives or parsley for garnish

Heat first amount of milk in large heavy saucepan.

Sauté onion in butter until clear and soft. Put into cone-shaped ricer.

Add corn to onion. Press through cone ricer. If you don't have a cone-shaped ricer, onion and corn may be puréed in blender. Rub through strainer if it isn't smooth enough.

Mix second amount of milk with flour, salt and pepper until no lumps remain. Stir into hot milk until it boils and thickens. Add corn and onion mixture. Heat through.

Serve with a dab of butter, chopped chives or parsley. Makes about 7 1/2 cups (1.9 L).

1 cup (250 mL): 129 Calories; 2.1 g Total Fat (0.7 g Mono, trace Poly, 1.1 g Sat); 9 mg Cholesterol; 22 g Carbohydrate; 1 g Fibre; 6 g Protein; 639 mg Sodium

Quick Broccoli Soup *A Classic!*

Can of condensed cream of mushroom soup	10 oz.	284 mL
Milk (1 soup can)	10 oz.	284 mL
Grated sharp Cheddar cheese	1 cup	250 mL
Frozen chopped broccoli, thawed, chopped into tiny bits	1 cup	250 mL
Worcestershire sauce	1/4 tsp.	1 mL

Stir soup and milk vigorously in large saucepan. Heat on medium for about 8 minutes, stirring often, until heated through.

Add cheese, broccoli and Worcestershire sauce. Heat for about 5 minutes, stirring often, until simmering. Reduce heat to medium-low. Simmer, uncovered, for about 5 minutes until broccoli is tender. Makes 4 1/2 cups (1.1 L).

1 cup (250 mL): 197 Calories; 12.7 g Total Fat (2.6 g Mono, 0.2 g Poly, 6.5 Sat); 33 mg Cholesterol; 11 g Carbohydrate; 2 g Fibre; 11 g Protein; 651 mg Sodium

Pictured below.

A cheese and broccoli soup that is easy to prepare, and thick and satisfying to eat.

serving suggestion

Serve this soup up in big mugs with warm biscuits on the side. Garnish with some grated Cheddar cheese.

Roasting the cauliflower adds a rich dimension to this creamy-textured soup, every bowl accented with a tangy red pepper drizzle.

Roasted Cauliflower Soup

Cauliflower florets	8 cups	2 L
Olive oil	2 tbsp.	30 mL
Dried thyme	1/4 tsp.	1 mL
Salt	1/2 tsp.	2 mL
Pepper	1/4 tsp.	1 mL
Prepared vegetable broth	3 cups	750 mL
Roasted red peppers	1/2 cup	125 mL
Prepared vegetable broth	1 tbsp.	15 mL
Dried basil	1/4 tsp.	1 mL

Preheat oven to 450°F (230°C). Put cauliflower into large bowl. Drizzle with olive oil. Sprinkle with next 3 ingredients. Toss until coated. Transfer to large ungreased baking sheet with sides. Spread evenly. Bake for about 15 minutes, stirring at halftime, until tender and starting to brown.

Meanwhile, measure first amount of broth into medium saucepan. Bring to a boil. Reduce heat to low. Cover to keep hot.

Put remaining 3 ingredients into blender or food processor. Process until smooth. Transfer to small cup. Rinse blender. Put cauliflower into blender. Add 2 cups (500 mL) hot broth. Process until smooth (see Safety Tip). Add to remaining hot broth. Stir. Makes about 5 1/2 cups (1.4 L) soup. Ladle into 4 soup bowls. Drizzle with red pepper mixture. Serves 4.

1 serving: 214 Calories; 8.0 g Total Fat (5.0 g Mono, 0.9 g Poly, 1.0 g Sat); trace Cholesterol; 31 g Carbohydrate; 13 g Fibre; 10 g Protein; 896 mg Sodium

Pictured at right.

Safety Tip: Follow manufacturer's instructions for processing hot liquids.

This sweet, velvety soup is simple to prepare but has such sophisticated flavours. Your guests will never guess how easy it is to make.

Caramelized Onion Sweet Potato Soup

Butter (or hard margarine)	1/4 cup	60 mL
Coarsely chopped onion	4 cups	1 L
Brown sugar, packed	1 tbsp.	15 mL
Coarsely chopped fresh peeled orange-fleshed sweet potato (about 1 lb., 454 g)	3 cups	750 mL
Prepared chicken broth	3 cups	750 mL
Dry sherry	2 tbsp.	30 mL
Dried thyme	1/4 tsp.	1 mL
Ground allspice	1/4 tsp.	1 mL
Salt	1/8 tsp.	0.5 mL
Pepper	1/4 tsp.	1 mL

Melt butter in large saucepan on medium. Add onion and brown sugar. Cook, uncovered, for about 30 minutes, stirring occasionally, until onion is caramelized.

Add remaining 7 ingredients. Stir. Bring to a boil. Reduce heat to medium-low. Simmer, covered, for about 20 minutes, stirring occasionally, until sweet potato is tender. Carefully process with hand blender or in blender until smooth (see Safety Tip). Makes about 5 cups (1.25 L). Serves 4.

1 serving: 270 Calories; 12.5 g Total Fat (3.3 g Mono, 0.9 g Poly, 7.5 g Sat); 30 mg Cholesterol; 37 g Carbohydrate; 5 g Fibre; 4 g Protein; 1301 mg Sodium

Pictured at right.

Safety Tip: Follow manufacturer's instructions for processing hot liquids.

Butternut squash is perfectly partnered with leek and potatoes in this rich, velvety-textured soup.

make ahead

Store in an airtight container in the freezer for up to 1 month. Thaw overnight in the refrigerator. Reheat the soup in a large pot or Dutch oven on medium heat for about 30 minutes, stirring occasionally, until heated through.

Silky Butternut Squash Soup

Cooking oil	1 tbsp.	15 mL
Thinly sliced leek (white part only)	1 1/2 cups	375 mL
Ground ginger	1 tbsp.	15 mL
Garlic cloves, minced (or 3/4 tsp., 4 mL, powder)	3	3
Chopped peeled butternut squash	10 cups	2.5 L
Chopped peeled potato	4 1/2 cups	1.1 L
Prepared chicken broth	8 cups	2 L
Pepper	1/2 tsp.	2 mL

Heat cooking oil in large pot or Dutch oven on medium. Add next 3 ingredients. Stir. Cook for about 5 minutes, stirring often, until leek is softened.

Add remaining 4 ingredients. Stir. Bring to a boil. Reduce heat to medium-low. Simmer, covered, for about 20 minutes, stirring occasionally, until squash and potato are softened. Remove from heat. Let stand for about 10 minutes until slightly cooled. Process squash mixture with hand blender (or in blender or food processor in small batches) until smooth (see Safety Tip). Heat and stir on medium for about 5 minutes until heated through. Makes about 16 cups (4 L). Serves 12.

1 serving: 151 Calories; 2.4 g Total Fat (1.1 g Mono, 0.6 g Poly, 0.4 g Sat); 0 mg Cholesterol; 28 g Carbohydrate; 3 g Fibre; 6 g Protein; 558 mg Sodium

Pictured at right.

Safety Tip: Follow manufacturer's instructions for processing hot liquids.

The perfect blend of pumpkin and spices! This thick pumpkin and apple soup, served with slices of whole-wheat bread, is just what you need on a chilly fall day.

about canned pumpkin

Be careful to purchase the right type of canned pumpkin that your recipe calls for. Pure pumpkin is just that—pumpkin with nothing added. Pumpkin pie filling, on the other hand, is pumpkin that has been blended with sugar and spices.

Autumn Pumpkin Soup

Olive (or canola) oil	2 tsp.	10 mL
Chopped onion	1 1/2 cups	375 mL
Low-sodium prepared chicken (or vegetable) broth	4 cups	1 L
Can of pure pumpkin (no spices)	14 oz.	398 mL
Unsweetened applesauce	1 cup	250 mL
Bay leaf	1	1
Chopped fresh thyme (or 1/2 tsp., 2 mL, dried)	2 tsp.	10 mL
Lemon pepper	1 tsp.	5 mL
Salt, sprinkle		

Heat olive oil in large saucepan on medium. Add onion. Cook for 5 to 10 minutes, stirring occasionally, until softened and starting to brown.

Add remaining 7 ingredients. Stir. Bring to a boil. Reduce heat to medium-low. Simmer, partially covered, for 10 minutes to blend flavours. Discard bay leaf. Makes about 7 cups (1.75 L).

1 cup (250 mL): 72 Calories; 1.9 g Total Fat (1.2 g Mono, 0.2 g Poly, 0.4 g Sat); 0 mg Cholesterol; 13 g Carbohydrate; 3 g Fibre; 2 g Protein; 42 mg Sodium

Pictured at right.

Who wouldn't be mellow after supping on this sunny, golden split-pea soup? This sweet vegetable blend has a delicious hint of dill.

about sweet potatoes

Sweet potatoes are related to morning glories, which are native to Central America, but their name is misleading because they're not related to potatoes. The kind commonly found in North America has orange or yellow flesh and is soft and moist when cooked. Although they are sometimes called yams, sweet potatoes are not true yams, which are tubers native to Africa and east Asia and not often found in local supermarkets.

about yellow zucchini

Yellow zucchini is essentially the same vegetable as green zucchini—it's simply a different variety, just as tomatoes come in many varieties that look different from each other. If yellow zucchini is not available, use peeled green zucchini.

Mellow Yellow Soup

Cooking oil	2 tsp.	10 mL
Chopped onion	1 cup	250 mL
Grated carrot	1 cup	250 mL
Vegetable (or chicken) broth	6 cups	1.5 L
Chopped yellow zucchini (with peel)	1 1/2 cups	375 mL
Chopped, peeled sweet potato (or yam)	1 cup	250 mL
Frozen kernel corn	1 cup	250 mL
Yellow split peas, rinsed and drained	3/4 cup	175 mL
Dill weed	1/2 tsp.	2 mL
Turmeric	1/4 tsp.	1 mL
Dried thyme	1/4 tsp.	1 mL
Bay leaf	1	1

Heat cooking oil in large saucepan on medium. Add onion and carrot. Cook for 5 to 10 minutes, stirring often, until onion is softened.

Add remaining 9 ingredients. Stir. Bring to a boil. Reduce heat to medium-low. Simmer, covered, for about 1 hour, stirring occasionally, until sweet potato is tender and split peas are very soft. Discard bay leaf. Makes about 8 cups (2 L).

1 cup (250 mL): 101 Calories; 1.9 g Total Fat (0.8 g Mono, 0.5 g Poly, 0.5 g Sat); 0 mg Cholesterol; 18 g Carbohydrate; 3 g Fibre; 5 g Protein; 700 mg Sodium

Lemon Lentil Soup

Olive (or cooking) oil	1 tbsp.	15 mL
Diced onion	1 1/2 cups	375 mL
Diced carrot	1 cup	250 mL
Chopped fresh oregano	1 1/2 tbsp.	25 mL
(or 1 1/4 tsp., 6 mL, dried)		
Garlic cloves, minced	3	3
Chopped fresh rosemary (or 1/4 tsp.,	1 tsp.	5 mL
1 mL, dried, crushed)		
Salt	1/2 tsp.	2 mL
Pepper	1/2 tsp.	2 mL
Dried crushed chilies	1/4 tsp.	1 mL
Bay leaf	1	1
Chicken Stock (page 26), or prepared	6 cups	1.5 L
chicken broth		
Dried red split lentils	1 1/2 cups	375 mL
Lemon juice	6 tbsp.	100 mL
Grated lemon zest (see Tip, page 104)	1 tsp.	5 mL
Pepper	1/8 tsp.	0.5 mL
Crumbled feta cheese	1/4 cup	60 mL
Chopped fresh parsley	1/4 cup	60 mL

Heat olive oil in large saucepan on medium-high. Add onion. Cook for 5 to 10 minutes, stirring often, until onion starts to brown.

Add next 8 ingredients. Cook for about 3 minutes, stirring often, until carrot is tender-crisp.

Add chicken stock and lentils. Bring to a boil. Reduce heat to medium-low. Simmer, partially covered, for about 20 minutes, stirring occasionally, until lentils are very soft. Discard bay leaf.

Stir in next 3 ingredients.

Sprinkle feta cheese and parsley on individual servings. Makes about 7 cups (1.75 L).

1 cup (250 mL): 228 Calories; 4.3 g Total Fat (1.8 g Mono, 0.5 g Poly, 1.7 g Sat); 5 mg Cholesterol; 35 g Carbohydrate; 6 g Fibre; 15 g Protein; 995 mg Sodium

This vibrant Mediterranean-inspired soup offers a fresh lemon background for a delightful spectrum of flavours.

about lentils

Lentils are tiny legumes available in many varieties, including brown, green, red and yellow. Rich in protein and carbohydrates, lentils are an ideal substitute for meat and are therefore a staple in vegetarian diets. They are dried after ripening, and are always eaten cooked.

Different and delicious—not your everyday potato soup! Leek and lemon enhance sweet pear to give this soup an intriguing elegance.

about cooking with pears

When cooking or baking with pears, it may be important to use firm, not-quite-ripe fruit that will hold its shape. Since this soup is pureed until smooth, feel free to use your favourite variety of this delectably juicy fruit—pears at their peak will offer all the more flavour.

tip

When a recipe calls for grated zest and juice, it's easier to grate the fruit first, then juice it. Be careful not to grate down to the pith (white part of the peel), which is bitter and best avoided.

Potato Pear Soup

Olive oil	2 tsp.	10 mL
Chopped peeled pear	3 cups	750 mL
Sliced leek (white part only)	1 cup	250 mL
Chopped peeled potato	3 cups	750 mL
Low-sodium prepared chicken broth	3 cups	750 mL
Pepper	1/8 tsp.	0.5 mL
Lemon juice	1 tbsp.	15 mL
Grated lemon zest (see Tip, left)	1/2 tsp.	2 mL

Heat olive oil in large saucepan on medium. Add pear and leek. Cook for about 5 minutes, stirring often, until leek is softened.

Add next 3 ingredients. Stir. Bring to a boil. Reduce heat to medium-low. Simmer, covered, for about 10 minutes until potato is soft. Carefully process with hand blender or in blender until smooth (see Safety Tip).

Stir in lemon juice and lemon zest. Makes about 6 cups (1.5 L).

1 cup (250 mL): 148 Calories; 2.1 g Total Fat (1.3 g Mono, 0.3 g Poly, 0.3 g Sat); 0 mg Cholesterol; 31 g Carbohydrate; 4 g Fibre; 3 g Protein; 26 mg Sodium

Safety Tip: Follow manufacturer's instructions for processing hot liquids.

Fennel and Grapefruit Soup

Canola oil	2 tsp.	10 mL
Chopped fennel bulb (white part only)	2 cups	500 mL
Chopped onion	1/2 cup	125 mL
Garlic clove, minced	1	1
(or 1/4 tsp., 1 mL, powder)		
Fennel seeds	1/2 tsp.	2 mL
Ground ginger	1/4 tsp.	1 mL
Brown sugar, packed	1 tsp.	5 mL
Low-sodium prepared chicken broth	2 cups	500 mL
Red grapefruit juice	1/4 cup	60 mL
Instant potato flakes	1/2 cup	125 mL
2% evaporated milk	1/2 cup	125 mL

Sliced green onion, for garnish

Heat canola oil in large saucepan on medium. Add next 5 ingredients. Cook for about 10 minutes, stirring often, until fennel and onion start to brown.

Add sugar. Heat and stir for about 1 minute until fennel and onion are golden.

Add broth and juice. Stir. Bring to a boil. Add potato flakes. Heat and stir until boiling and thickened. Add evaporated milk. Cook and stir until heated through. Carefully process with hand blender or in blender until smooth (see Safety Tip).

Garnish with green onion. Makes about 4 cups (1 L). Serves 4.

1 serving: 158 Calories; 3.4 g Total Fat (1.6 g Mono, 0.7 g Poly, 0.6 g Sat); 5 mg Cholesterol; 28 g Carbohydrate; 7 g Fibre; 7 g Protein; 441 mg Sodium

Safety Tip: Follow manufacturer's instructions for processing hot liquids.

Ready to try something completely new? Caramelizing onion and fennel brings out a natural sweetness that is brightened by tart grapefruit juice. These flavours go surprisingly well together!

This twist on traditional vichyssoise forgoes regular potatoes for sweet potatoes, giving it a unique flavour that's far from ordinary. The lime sour cream adds a delectable kick.

lime sour cream

Sour cream	1/3 cup	75 mL
Lime juice	1 tbsp.	15 mL
Grated lime zest	1 tsp.	5 mL
(see Tip, page 104)		

Stir all 3 ingredients in small bowl. Drizzle onto individual servings of soup. Makes about 1/3 cup (75 mL).

about sweet potato

There is much confusion regarding sweet potatoes and yams. Some are orange-fleshed, while others are white-fleshed. For this recipe, we've used a white-fleshed sweet potato, but the orange-fleshed ones will work just as well!

Sweet Potato Vichyssoise

Butter (or hard margarine)	3 tbsp.	50 mL
Chopped peeled sweet potato	2 1/2 cups	625 mL
Sliced leek (white part only)	2 cups	500 mL
Chicken Stock (page 26), or prepared chicken broth	4 cups	1 L
Chopped fresh thyme (or 1/2 tsp., 2 mL, dried)	2 tsp.	10 mL
Salt	1/2 tsp.	2 mL
Pepper	1/2 tsp.	2 mL
Whipping cream	1/2 cup	125 mL

Heat butter in large saucepan on medium until melted. Add sweet potato and leek. Cook for about 5 minutes, stirring occasionally, until leek is softened.

Add next 4 ingredients. Stir. Bring to a boil. Reduce heat to medium-low. Simmer, partially covered, for about 20 minutes, stirring occasionally, until sweet potato is tender.

Add whipping cream. Carefully process with hand blender or in blender until smooth (see Safety Tip). Transfer to large bowl. Cool at room temperature before covering. Chill for at least 2 hours until cold. Makes 6 cups (1.5 L). Serves 6.

1 serving with 2 1/2 tsp. (12 mL) Lime Sour Cream: 228 Calories; 15.1 g Total Fat (4.2 g Mono, 0.6 g Poly, 9.4 g Sat); 45 mg Cholesterol; 21 g Carbohydrate; 3 g Fibre; 4 g Protein; 857 mg Sodium

Pictured at right.

Safety Tip: Follow manufacturer's instructions for processing hot liquids.

The texture of pureed wild rice combines with the fresh flavours of avocado and cucumber. Sure to infuse some cool into the hottest summer day. Try garnishing with a spoon of salsa for a spicy twist.

Avocado Rice Soup

Chopped avocado	1 1/2 cups	375 mL
Lemon juice	2 tbsp.	30 mL
Prepared vegetable broth	3 cups	750 mL
Ground cumin	1/4 tsp.	1 mL
Wild rice	1/3 cup	75 mL
Chopped peeled English cucumber, seeds removed	1 cup	250 mL
Milk	1/2 cup	125 mL
Lemon juice	1 tbsp.	15 mL
Salt	1/2 tsp.	2 mL
Pepper	1/4 tsp.	1 mL

Toss avocado and lemon juice in medium bowl. Set aside.

Combine broth and cumin in medium saucepan. Bring to a boil. Add wild rice. Stir. Reduce heat to medium-low. Simmer, covered, for about 75 minutes until wild rice is tender. Remove from heat.

Add remaining 5 ingredients and avocado mixture. Carefully process with hand blender or in blender until smooth (see Safety Tip). Pour into large bowl. Cool to room temperature. Chill, covered, for about 3 hours until cold. Makes about 5 cups (1.25 L).

1 cup (250 mL): 134 Calories; 7.1 g Total Fat (4.5 g Mono, 0.9 g Poly, 1.1 g Sat); 1 mg Cholesterol; 16 g Carbohydrate; 4 g Fibre; 4 g Protein; 533 mg Sodium

Pictured at right.

Safety Tip: Follow manufacturer's instructions for processing hot liquids

A creamy blend of potato and leek, Vichyssoise (vihsh-ee-SWAHZ) is best when served very cold.

Vichyssoise   *A Classic!*

Peeled, cubed potatoes	4 cups	1 L
Leeks (white part only), cut up	3	3
Medium onion, sliced	1	1
Parsley flakes	1 tsp.	5 mL
Salt	1 tsp.	5 mL
Pepper	1/4 tsp.	1 mL
Ground nutmeg, sprinkle		
Can of condensed chicken broth	10 oz.	284 mL
Water	1 3/4 cups	425 mL

(continued on next page)

| Skim evaporated milk (or light cream) | 2/3 cup | 150 mL |
| Milk | 1 cup | 250 mL |

Chopped chives, for garnish

Combine first 9 ingredients in large saucepan. Cook until vegetables are tender. Do not drain. Purée in blender (see Safety Tip). Pour into large bowl.

Stir in both milks. Cover. Chill for several hours.

Sprinkle chives on top. Makes 8 cups (2 L).

1 cup (250 mL): 112 Calories; 0.7 g Total Fat (0.1 g Mono, trace Poly, 0.2 g Sat); 3 mg Cholesterol; 22 g Carbohydrate; 2 g Fibre; 4 g Protein; 567 mg Sodium

Safety Tip: Follow manufacturer's instructions for processing hot liquids.

Avocado Rice Soup, left

food fun

Although some argue that vichyssoise is a classic French soup invented in France in the 1800s and originally served hot, others believe that it was invented by French chef Louis Diat in New York in 1930 and named after his home town, Vichy. A third argument provides a compromise—claiming that Diat altered an old French recipe for hot soup so it could be served chilled.

This sweet and refreshing soup is wonderfully balanced with tangy dill and buttermilk. Try serving it with Herbed Tortillas for dunking.

herbed tortillas

Flour tortillas (9 inch, 23 cm, diameter)	2	2
Olive (or cooking) oil	1 tsp.	5 mL
Italian seasoning	1 tsp.	5 mL
Dried crushed chilies	1/2 tsp.	2 mL

Brush tortillas with olive oil. Combine Italian seasoning and chilies in small cup. Sprinkle over tortillas. Cut into 8 wedges each. Arrange wedges on greased baking sheet. Bake in 350°F (175°C) oven for about 10 minutes until crisp and lightly browned. Serve with soup. Makes 16 wedges.

Pictured at right.

Chilled Pea Dill Soup

Cooking oil	1 tsp.	5 mL
Chopped celery	1 cup	250 mL
Chopped onion	1 cup	250 mL
Garlic clove, minced (or 1/4 tsp., 1 mL, powder)	1	1
Salt	1/2 tsp.	2 mL
Pepper	1/4 tsp.	1 mL
Prepared vegetable broth	2 cups	500 mL
Frozen peas	2 cups	500 mL
Dried dillweed	2 tsp.	10 mL
Buttermilk	1 1/2 cups	375 mL

Heat cooking oil in large saucepan or Dutch oven on medium. Add next 5 ingredients. Cook, uncovered, for 5 to 10 minutes, stirring often, until onion is softened.

Add broth. Bring to a boil.

Add peas and dill. Bring to a boil. Reduce heat to medium. Boil gently, uncovered, for 3 to 5 minutes until peas are tender. Carefully process with hand blender or in blender until smooth (see Safety Tip). Pour into large bowl.

Add buttermilk. Stir. Chill for 2 hours. Makes about 5 cups (1.25 L) soup. Serves 4.

1 serving with 4 Herbed Tortilla wedges: 217 Calories; 5.7 g Total Fat (1.8 g Mono, 0.7 g Poly, 1.3 g Sat); 3 mg Cholesterol; 33 g Carbohydrate; 5 g Fibre; 10 g Protein; 881 mg Sodium

Pictured at right.

Safety Tip: Follow manufacturer's instructions for processing hot liquids.

Left: Chilled Pea Dill Soup, above
Right: Herbed Tortillas, left

Borscht by any other name is still beet soup—but this chilled version delivers a whole new taste sensation.

Chilled Beet Soup

Cans of whole baby beets (14 oz., 398 mL, each), with liquid	2	2
Prepared vegetable broth, chilled	1 1/2 cups	375 mL
Light sour cream	1/2 cup	125 mL
Chopped green onion	1/3 cup	75 mL
Chopped fresh dill (or 1 tbsp., 15 mL, dried)	1/4 cup	60 mL
Dill pickle juice	2 tbsp.	30 mL
Granulated sugar	1 tbsp.	15 mL
Pepper	1/4 tsp.	1 mL
Chopped dill pickle	2 tbsp.	30 mL

Put beets into large bowl. Mash until beets are crushed. Add next 7 ingredients. Stir well.

Stir in pickle. Makes about 6 cups (1.5 L). Serves 4.

1 serving: 122 Calories; 2.9 g Total Fat (trace Mono, trace Poly, 1.5 g Sat); 10 mg Cholesterol; 21 g Carbohydrate; 3 g Fibre; 4 g Protein; 896 mg Sodium

Pictured at right.

You'll love the refreshing dill and cucumber flavours in this deep red, easy-to-make chilled soup. Serve with a dollop of sour cream for an attractive finish.

Gazpacho

Medium tomatoes, peeled and coarsely chopped	6	6
English cucumber (with peel), coarsely chopped	1	1
Coarsely chopped red onion	3/4 cup	175 mL
Garlic cloves, minced (or 1/2 tsp., 2 mL, powder)	2	2
Chopped fresh dill (or 1 1/2 tsp., 7 mL, dill weed)	2 tbsp.	30 mL
Balsamic vinegar	2 tbsp.	30 mL
Granulated sugar	1 tsp.	5 mL
Hot pepper sauce	1 tsp.	5 mL
Salt	1/2 tsp.	2 mL
Coarsely ground pepper (or sprinkle of pepper)	1/4 tsp.	1 mL

(continued on next page)

| Tomato juice | 19 oz. | 540 mL |
| Large avocado, finely chopped | 1 | 1 |

Put first 10 ingredients into food processor. Pulse with on/off motion for about 20 seconds until finely chopped. Put into large bowl.

Add tomato juice. Stir. Cover. Chill for at least 3 hours or overnight.

Scatter avocado over individual servings. Makes about 7 1/2 cups (1.9 L).

1 cup (250 mL): 95 Calories; 4.3 g Total Fat (2.7 g Mono, 0.7 g Poly, 0.6 g Sat); 0 mg Cholesterol; 14 g Carbohydrate; 4 g Fibre; 3 g Protein; 375 mg Sodium

Pictured below.

Left: Gazpacho, left
Right: Chilled Beet Soup, left

Put a tropical spin on gazpacho with mango, shrimp and lime. When tomatoes are in season, this recipe is a great way to use up the overripe ones—just replace the canned tomatoes in the recipe with fresh.

about gazpacho

This summertime refresher has very rustic origins in the Andalusia region of Spain. It began as labourers' food made of simple, portable ingredients—bread and vegetables. In Spain, it has several variations: topped with raw onion rings or grapes and almonds, made with a veal bouillon or mayonnaise base, thickened with cream and cornstarch or flavoured with cumin and basil. Modern gazpacho can include such a wide variety of ingredients that the word itself is often used as a generic term for chilled vegetable soup.

South Seas Gazpacho

Can of diced tomatoes (with juice)	28 oz.	796 mL
Chopped English cucumber (with peel)	1 cup	250 mL
Chopped red pepper	1/2 cup	125 mL
Chopped onion	1/4 cup	60 mL
Chopped frozen mango pieces, thawed	1 1/2 cups	375 mL
Lime juice	2 tbsp.	30 mL
Chopped fresh dill (or 1 tsp., 5 mL dried)	4 tsp.	20 mL
Olive oil	1 tbsp.	15 mL
Celery salt	1/2 tsp.	2 mL
Grated lime zest (see Tip, page 104)	1/2 tsp.	2 mL
Chopped cooked salad shrimp	1 3/4 cups	425 mL
Sour cream	1/4 cup	60 mL
Mayonnaise	3 tbsp.	50 mL
Chopped fresh cilantro (or parsley)	1 tsp.	5 mL
Grated lime zest	1/4 tsp.	1 mL

Process first 4 ingredients in food processor with on/off motion until almost smooth. Transfer to large bowl.

Process next 6 ingredients until smooth. Add to tomato mixture. Stir. Chill, covered, for at least 2 hours to blend flavours.

Add shrimp. Stir. Ladle into 6 chilled serving bowls.

Combine remaining 4 ingredients in small bowl. Spoon about 1 tbsp. (15 mL) over each serving. Makes 6 cups (1.5 L). Serves 6.

1 serving: 231 Calories; 14.6 g Total Fat (3.0 g Mono, 2.9 g Poly, 3.0 g Sat); 69 mg Cholesterol; 17 g Carbohydrate; 1 g Fibre; 10 g Protein; 601 mg Sodium

Pictured at right.

This chilled soup is Scandinavian in origin, made with simple ingredients that are easy to keep on hand. Serve as a starter soup or as a light dessert.

serving suggestion

Fruit Soup looks elegant served in martini glasses or small soup bowls in contrasting colours. Garnish with mint or a light sprinkling of cinnamon.

Fruit Soup   *A Classic!*

Water	4 cups	1 L
Pineapple juice	2 1/4 cups	550 mL
Chopped mixed dried fruit (prunes, apricots, apples, peaches), lightly packed	2 cups	500 mL
Raisins or currants	1/2 cup	125 mL
Orange juice	1/2 cup	125 mL
Cinnamon	1/4 tsp.	1 mL
Granulated sugar	1/3 cup	75 mL
Minute tapioca	2 tbsp.	30 mL

Put water and pineapple juice into large saucepan. Add remaining ingredients. Bring to a boil over medium heat. Cover. Simmer gently for 30 minutes. Cool. Serve chilled. Makes 4 cups (1 L).

1 cup (250 mL): 406 Calories; 0.5 g Total Fat (0.2 g Mono, 0.1 g Poly, trace Sat); 0 mg Cholesterol; 105 g Carbohydrate; 7 g Fibre; 3 g Protein; 23 mg Sodium

A smooth and refreshing cantaloupe purèe topped off with a fun sprinkle of blueberries—perfect for enjoying on the patio with a summertime brunch.

about dessert tofu

What's dessert tofu? Tofu comes in several varieties that differ in firmness, the softest of which is called silken tofu. This type has the highest moisture content and a fine, soft, custard-like texture. Dessert tofu is very much like silken tofu, but with different flavours and sweeteners added to it. You can add it to recipes or eat it as a snack on its own.

Frosty Fruit Soup

Frozen chopped cantaloupe	1 cup	250 mL
Tropical fruit juice	3/4 cup	175 mL
Peach dessert tofu	1/3 cup	75 mL
Fresh (or frozen) blueberries	1/4 cup	60 mL

Put the first 3 ingredients into the blender. Cover with the lid. Process until smooth. Pour into the bowl.

Scatter the blueberries over top. Serves 1.

1 serving: 263 Calories; 4.9 g Total Fat (0.9 g Mono, 2.4 g Poly, 0.6 g Sat); 0 mg Cholesterol; 50 g Carbohydrate; 3 g Fibre; 9 g Protein; 26 mg Sodium

Pictured at right.

Frosty Fruit Soup, above

Serve up a taste of summer at your next outdoor party! Arrange the serving bowl on a bed of ice, surrounding it with fresh fruit slices for an inviting presentation.

potluck suggestion

This dessert soup serves up to 16, making it perfect for a large gathering.

West Indies Summer Soup

Diced cantaloupe	4 cups	1 L
Diced ripe mango	2 cups	500 mL
Orange juice	2 cups	500 mL
Plain yogurt	1 cup	250 mL
Lime juice	2 tbsp.	30 mL
Liquid honey	2 tbsp.	30 mL
Ground ginger	1 tsp.	5 mL
Ground cinnamon	1/2 tsp.	2 mL

Process all 8 ingredients in blender, in batches, or food processor until smooth. Transfer to large serving bowl. Chill for at least 2 hours until cold. Makes about 8 cups (2 L).

1 cup (250 mL): 126 Calories; 1 g Total Fat (0.2 g Mono, 0.1 g Poly, 0.4 g Sat); 2 mg Cholesterol; 29 g Carbohydrate; 2 g Fibre; 3 g Protein; 32 mg Sodium

Pictured at right.

This sweet treat makes a perfect palate cleanser between courses, or a refreshing dessert. Serve it in punch cups for extra style points.

about mango

North Americans often think of the mango mainly as a sweet fruit, but in tropical cuisines it plays a more diverse role. The young leaves and shoots of the mango tree are eaten with spicy chili relishes; unripe and semi-ripe mangoes are pickled, made into relishes or eaten raw with salt and chillies; and ripe mangoes are eaten on their own, with or in curries, as a sun-dried snack or as a dessert purée.

Pineapple Mango Soup

Cans of sliced mango (with syrup), (14 oz., 398 mL, each)	2	2
Chopped fresh pineapple	6 cups	1.5 L
Canned coconut milk	1/2 cup	125 mL

Process all 3 ingredients in blender, in batches, or food processor until smooth. Press through sieve into large bowl. Discard solids. Stir. Chill, covered, for at least 2 hours until cold. Makes about 6 cups (1.5 L).

1 cup (250 mL): 237 Calories; 5.2 g Total Fat (0.3 g Mono, 0.3 g Poly, 3.9 g Sat); 0 mg Cholesterol; 52 g Carbohydrate; 3 g Fibre; 1 g Protein; 34 mg Sodium

Pictured at right.

Left: Pineapple Mango Soup, above
Right: West Indies Summer Soup, above

Similar to a cheery apple cider, this is a clear, golden soup with a bit of apple texture.

Apple Soup is attractive when garnished with a cinnamon stick over each bowl.

Apple Soup

Apple juice	4 cups	1 L
Apples, peeled, cored and diced	4	4
Cinnamon	1/2 tsp.	2 mL
Lemon juice	1 tsp.	5 mL
Brown sugar, packed	1/2 cup	125 mL
Cinnamon sticks (optional)		

Simmer all together, covered, in large pot until apples are barely tender. Chill. Serve cold. Makes 5 1/2 cups (1.4 L).

1 cup (250 mL): 191 Calories; 0.1 g Total Fat (trace Mono, trace Poly, trace Sat); 0 mg Cholesterol; 51 g Carbohydrate; 1 g Fibre; trace Protein; 7 mg Sodium

Pictured at right.

There is a pleasing tartness to this cool summer soup, which looks lovely served with a sour cream or whipped cream garnish. It's easily doubled or tripled.

Cherry Soup

Can of pitted Bing cherries in heavy syrup	14 oz.	398 mL
Red wine vinegar	1 tbsp.	15 mL
Granulated sugar	2 tsp.	10 mL
Ground cinnamon	1/8 tsp.	0.5 mL
Salt sprinkle (optional)		
Sour cream, whipped cream or heavy cream (for garnish)		

Add cherries with syrup and next 4 ingredients to blender. Blend until smooth. Chill.

Serve with a dab of sour cream or plain whipped cream, or pour a bit of heavy cream in center of bowl. Swirl with spoon. Makes about 1 3/4 cups (425 mL).

1/2 cup (125 mL): 100 Calories; 0.2 g Total Fat (0.1 g Mono, 0.1 g Poly, trace Sat); 0 mg Cholesterol; 26 g Carbohydrate; 2 g Fibre; 1 g Protein; 3 mg Sodium

Pictured at right.

Left: Apple Soup, above
Right: Cherry Soup, above

Indulge in the summer-fresh strawberry taste and hint of citrus in this vibrantly red, refreshing soup.

tip

Use fresh local strawberries when they are in season for the best possible flavour.

Strawberry Soup

Granulated sugar	3/4 cup	175 mL
Water	1 1/2 cups	375 mL
Fresh strawberries, halved (about 1 1/2 lbs., 680 g)	4 cups	1 L
Grated lemon zest	1 1/2 tsp.	7 mL
Grated orange zest	2 tsp.	10 mL
Sherry (or fresh orange juice)	1/4 cup	60 mL
Whipping cream (optional)	4 tsp.	20 mL

Combine sugar and water in small saucepan. Bring to a boil on medium, stirring occasionally. Reduce heat to medium-low. Simmer for 10 minutes. Cool.

Combine next 4 ingredients in large bowl. Add sugar mixture. Stir. Process, in 2 batches, in blender until smooth. Strain juice into large bowl. Discard seeds. Pour into container. Chill.

Garnish individual servings with swirls of whipping cream. Serve chilled. Makes 3 1/2 cups (875 mL). Serves 4.

1 serving: 154 Calories; 0.5 g Total Fat (0.1 g Mono, 0.2 g Poly, trace Sat); 0 mg Cholesterol; 41 g Carbohydrate; 3 g Fibre; 1 g Protein; 92 mg Sodium

Pictured below.

Strawberry Cucumber Soup

Coarsely chopped, peeled English cucumber, seeds removed	3 cups	750 mL
Frozen whole strawberries, partially thawed	3 cups	750 mL
White grape juice	1 cup	250 mL
Granulated sugar	1/4 cup	60 mL
Ground ginger	1 tsp.	5 mL
Ground cinnamon	1/4 tsp.	1 mL
Salt	1/4 tsp.	1 mL
Pepper	1/4 tsp.	1 mL
Half-and-half cream	1/2 cup	125 mL

Put cucumber into blender or food processor. Process until smooth.

Add next 7 ingredients. Process until almost smooth. Transfer to medium bowl.

Add cream. Stir. Chill. Makes about 5 1/2 cups (1.4 L). Serves 12.

1 serving: 58 Calories; 1.4 g Total Fat (0.4 g Mono, 0.1 g Poly, 0.8 g Sat); 4 mg Cholesterol; 11 g Carbohydrate; 1 g Fibre; 1 g Protein; 55 mg Sodium

Pictured below.

There's something so refined about a lovely chilled soup. This cool blend is mildly sweetened with cinnamon and ginger, and can be garnished with thin slices of cucumber or strawberries.

about fruit soups

Ever wonder where the idea to make a soup from fruit originated? It's not really clear who thought it up, but certain parts of the world do seem to be better known than others for their love of cold and warm fruit soups. The cuisines of Scandinavia, Russia, Eastern Europe, the Middle East, Baltic countries, central Asia and China all feature such soups, while those of Japan, South America, southeast Asia, the South Pacific, Africa and Western Europe generally don't.

serving suggestion

Try serving this soup in small punch glasses as a starter before a holiday dinner.

Throughout this book measurements are given in Conventional and Metric measure. To compensate for differences between the two measurements due to rounding, a full metric measure is not always used. The cup used is the standard 8 fluid ounce. Temperature is given in degrees Fahrenheit and Celsius. Baking pan measurements are in inches and centimetres as well as quarts and litres. An exact metric conversion is given on this page as well as the working equivalent (Metric Standard Measure).

Pans

Conventional – Inches	Metric – Centimetres
8 × 8 inch	20 × 20 cm
9 × 9 inch	23 × 23 cm
9 × 13 inch	23 × 33 cm
10 × 15 inch	25 × 38 cm
11 × 17 inch	28 × 43 cm
8 × 2 inch round	20 × 5 cm
9 × 2 inch round	23 × 5 cm
10 × 4 1/2 inch tube	25 × 11 cm
8 × 4 × 3 inch loaf	20 × 10 × 7.5 cm
9 × 5 × 3 inch loaf	23 × 12.5 × 7.5 cm

Oven Temperatures

Fahrenheit (°F)	Celsius (°C)	Fahrenheit (°F)	Celsius (°C)
175°	80°	350°	175°
200°	95°	375°	190°
225°	110°	400°	205°
250°	120°	425°	220°
275°	140°	450°	230°
300°	150°	475°	240°
325°	160°	500°	260°

Spoons

Conventional Measure	Metric Exact Conversion Millilitre (mL)	Metric Standard Measure Millilitre (mL)
1/8 teaspoon (tsp.)	0.6 mL	0.5 mL
1/4 teaspoon (tsp.)	1.2 mL	1 mL
1/2 teaspoon (tsp.)	2.4 mL	2 mL
1 teaspoon (tsp.)	4.7 mL	5 mL
2 teaspoons (tsp.)	9.4 mL	10 mL
1 tablespoon (tbsp.)	14.2 mL	15 mL

Cups

1/4 cup (4 tbsp.)	56.8 mL	60 mL
1/3 cup (5 1/3 tbsp.)	75.6 mL	75 mL
1/2 cup (8 tbsp.)	113.7 mL	125 mL
2/3 cup (10 2/3 tbsp.)	151.2 mL	150 mL
3/4 cup (12 tbsp.)	170.5 mL	175 mL
1 cup (16 tbsp.)	227.3 mL	250 mL
4 1/2 cups	1022.9 mL	1000 mL(1 L)

Dry Measurements

Conventional Measure Ounces (oz.)	Metric Exact Conversion Grams (g)	Metric Standard Measure Grams (g)
1 oz.	28.3 g	28 g
2 oz.	56.7 g	57 g
3 oz.	85.0 g	85 g
4 oz.	113.4 g	125 g
5 oz.	141.7 g	140 g
6 oz.	170.1 g	170 g
7 oz.	198.4 g	200 g
8 oz.	226.8 g	250 g
16 oz.	453.6 g	500 g
32 oz.	907.2 g	1000 g (1 kg)

Casseroles

Canada & Britain		United States	
Standard Size Casserole	Exact Metric Measure	Standard Size Casserole	Exact Metric Measure
1 qt. (5 cups)	1.13 L	1 qt. (4 cups)	900 mL
1 1/2 qts. (7 1/2 cups)	1.69 L	1 1/2 qts. (6 cups)	1.35 L
2 qts. (10 cups)	2.25 L	2 qts. (8 cups)	1.8 L
2 1/2 qts. (12 1/2 cups)	2.81 L	2 1/2 qts. (10 cups)	2.25 L
3 qts. (15 cups)	3.38 L	3 qts. (12 cups)	2.7 L
4 qts. (20 cups)	4.5 L	4 qts. (16 cups)	3.6 L
5 qts. (25 cups)	5.63 L	5 qts. (20 cups)	4.5 L

most loved recipe collection most loved recipe collection most loved recipe collection
loved recipe collection most loved recipe collection most loved recipe collection most
ction most loved recipe collection most loved recipe collection most loved recipe coll
most loved recipe collection most loved recipe collection most loved recipe collection
tion most loved recipe collection most loved recipe collection most loved recipe colle
most loved recipe collection most loved recipe collection most loved recipe collection
e collection most loved recipe collection most loved recipe collection most loved reci
ction most loved recipe collection most loved recipe collection most loved recipe coll
most loved recipe collection most loved recipe collection most loved recipe collection
loved recipe collection most loved recipe collection most loved recipe collection most
ction most loved recipe collection most loved recipe collection most loved recipe coll
most loved recipe collection most loved recipe collection most loved recipe collection
tion most loved recipe collection most loved recipe collection most loved recipe colle
most loved recipe collection most loved recipe collection most loved recipe collection
e collection most loved recipe collection most loved recipe collection most loved reci
ction most loved recipe collection most loved recipe collection most loved recipe coll
most loved recipe collection most loved recipe collection most loved recipe collection
loved recipe collection most loved recipe collection most loved recipe collection most
ction most loved recipe collection most loved recipe collection most loved recipe coll
most loved recipe collection most loved recipe collection most loved recipe collection
tion most loved recipe collection most loved recipe collection most loved recipe colle
most loved recipe collection most loved recipe collection most loved recipe collection
e collection most loved recipe collection most loved recipe collection most loved reci
ction most loved recipe collection most loved recipe collection most loved recipe coll
most loved recipe collection most loved recipe collection most loved recipe collection
loved recipe collection most loved recipe collection most loved recipe collection most
ction most loved recipe collection most loved recipe collection most loved recipe colle
most loved recipe collection most loved recipe collection most loved recipe collection
collection most loved recipe collection most loved recipe collection most loved recipe collection